Interventions is produced on the land of the Wurundjeri people of the Kulin Nation. We acknowledge the Traditional Owners of country throughout Australia and recognise their continuing connection to land, waters and culture. We pay our respects to their Elders past, present and emerging. Their land was stolen, never ceded.

It always was and always will be Aboriginal land.

First published 1998 by Interventions Publishers
2nd edition 2008 by Red Rag Publications
3rd edition 2022 by Interventions Inc

Interventions Inc is a not-for-profit, independent, radical book publisher. For further information:
www.interventions.org.au
info@interventions.org.au
PO Box 24132
Melbourne VIC 3001

Design and layout of cover and interior of this edition by Belle Gibson
Images used in cover design clockwise from top:
South Maitland Unemployed Women's Bureau practising banner carrying for May Day 1930s. Image courtesy of Coalfields Local History Association Inc, digitised by Special Collections, University of Newcastle, Australia.
Migrant women strikers at Kortex factory, Melbourne 1981. Image *The Battler* 23 January 1982 p 10.
Members of the New Housewives Association demonstrate with slogans painted on aprons Melbourne 1949. Photographer unknown. Image courtesy Anne Sgro.
Miss Mildred Thornton at a lathe in machine shop. Photographer unknown. State Library Victoria (H98.105/717).
Union of Australian Women demonstration for equal pay Melbourne early 1960s. Photographer Zillah Lee. Image courtesy of Anne Sgro.

Editors: Sandra Bloodworth and Tom O'Lincoln

Title: Rebel Women in Australian Working Class History
ISBN: 978-0-6452534-6-7: Paperback
ISBN: 978-0-6452534-7-4: ebook

© Sandra Bloodworth and Tom O'Lincoln 2022

The moral rights of the author have been asserted.
All rights reserved. Except as permitted under the Australian Copyright Act 1968 (for example, a fair dealing for the purposes of study, research, criticism or review), no part of this book may be reproduced, stored in a retrieval system, communicated or transmitted in any form or by any means without prior written permission.

All inquiries should be made to the publisher.

 A catalogue record for this work is available from the National Library of Australia

REBEL WOMEN

edited by
Sandra Bloodworth
& Tom O'Lincoln

INTERVENTIONS

This book is dedicated to all the named and unnamed women whose stories are told in these pages and to the present and future generations of working class women and their supporters who carry on the struggle.

Contents

Preface ... i
Introduction to the third edition ... 1
Introduction to the 1998 edition ... 7

1 **Militant Spirits:** *The rebel women of Broken Hill*
 Sandra Bloodworth ... 19
2 **Brazen hussies and God's police:** *Fighting back in the Depression years*
 Janey Stone ... 43
3 **Class struggle on the home front:** *Women, unions and militancy in the Second World War*
 Janey Stone ... 71
4 **Against the stream:** *Women and the left, 1945-1968*
 Tom O'Lincoln ... 103
5 **Militant action among white-collar workers:** *The struggle for equal pay in the insurance industry 1973-1975*
 Diane Fieldes ... 133
6 **Sweatshop Rebels:** *The 1981 Kortex strike*
 Sandra Bloodworth ... 155
7 **Dedication doesn't pay the rent!** *The 1986 Victorian nurses' strike*
 Liz Ross ... 169

Acronyms and abbreviations ... 187
Endnotes ... 189
Image credits ... 207
Contributors ... 213

Preface

Rebel Women was first published in 1998 and reprinted, virtually unchanged, in 2008. It has enjoyed steady sales over the last two decades and is now out of print. All chapters except for the last were originally published elsewhere. Previous publication details are:

Militant spirits – Sandra Bloodworth
Based on a thesis entitled *Rebel Women: Women and Class in Broken Hill, 1889–1917*, BA (Hons) diss., La Trobe University, 1996.

Brazen hussies and God's police – Janey Stone
An earlier version of this chapter appeared as 'Brazen Hussies and God's Police: Feminist Historiography and the Great Depression', *Hecate*, vol. VIII, no. 1, 1982.

Class struggle on the home front – Janey Stone
An earlier version of this chapter originally appeared as 'Women in the Metal Trades', *Front Line*, vol. 5, Melbourne, International Socialists, December 1976.

Against the stream – Tom O'Lincoln
An earlier version of this chapter appeared as 'Women and the Communist Party of Australia', *Hecate*, vol. VI, no. 1, 1980.

Militant action among white-collar workers – Diane Fieldes
An earlier version of this chapter appeared as '"Everybody Was 'Girls' in

the Minds of the Management": The Fight for Equal Pay in the Australian Insurance Industry, 1973-75', *Labour History*, vol. 73, November 1997.

Sweatshop rebels – Sandra Bloodworth

This chapter is based on Sandra Bloodworth's direct involvement with the strike, recounted in a talk at the 1982 Women and Labour Conference in Adelaide. The original published version was entitled 'Migrant Women Organise: The Kortex Strike of 1981', *Hecate*, vol. X, August 1983; later reprinted as a pamphlet, *Sweatshop Rebels*, Melbourne, Redback Press, 1983.

Dedication doesn't pay the rent! – Liz Ross

This chapter is based on Liz Ross' support of and involvement with the strike. An earlier version appeared as 'Sisters are Doing It for Themselves...and Us', *Hecate*, vol. XIII, no. 1, 1987; later reprinted as a pamphlet, *Dedication Doesn't Pay the Rent!*, Socialist Action, 1987.

It is striking to see that many of these were written in the 1970s and 1980s but retain their sparkle and interest decades later.

While researching the material for chapter 1, Sandra visited Broken Hill many times and developed strong bonds with many of the townspeople and unionists. She gave the keynote address at the launch in 2009 of the 1909 Lockout Centenary Exhibition. She talked about the 'determination and sacrifice of the people' in that dispute and explained how important it is to preserve and pass on this history, 'to learn lessons from it, to take courage from it.'[1]

Sandra noted that bosses still demand workers accept lower living standards, and support for unemployed people is poor:

> the centenary celebration isn't just about the past. It's about the fact that the class struggle is just as relevant today as it was then.

Rebel Women made a contribution to passing on this history – to the people of Broken Hill and to other interested workers.

In her new introduction, Liz Ross reveals how young women who have come to socialist ideas more recently have responded to this book.

This new edition retains the original introduction and chapters, with only minor alterations, but is now published in a modern, digitally based version enhanced by numerous images and illustrations. Produced using print-on-demand, this book will not sell out but will continue to be available to inspire new generations of activists into the future.

Thanks are due to Eris Harrison for compiling and copy editing a less than ideal set of files from a previous era and to Ian Syson of Vulgar Press for providing those files. We are grateful to Belle Gibson for her all-new design, particularly her work on presenting the Kortex strike. Kath Larkin brought a fresh interest to this same strike, and her contemporary interview with Bahriye Akalin reminds us of how the experience of militant struggle makes a permanent impression on participants. I thank Lisa Milner for personally encouraging me to pursue this new edition. Liz Ross provided a new introduction. Liz, Sandra Bloodworth and Diane Fieldes made their chapters available and provided input along the way. Robert Zocchi transcribed the speech Sandra made at the centenary of the 1909 lockout in Broken Hill.

We are also very grateful to the people whose financial assistance made this new edition possible: Graeme Haynes, Anne Lawson, Tess Lee-Ack, Dave Nadel, Tom O'Lincoln, Liz Ross, Robert Stainsby, Fleur Taylor, Phillip Whitefield and Robert Zocchi.

Lastly, I wish to mention Tom O'Lincoln. Ever since I was first with him in the USA in 1969, Tom encouraged my involvement in Women's Liberation. He himself wrote a number of articles on the subject of women's working-class struggles. The one that appears here was written in 1980 and was associated with his interest in the Communist Party of Australia (CPA). Those interested in this subject can read his book on the history of the CPA, *Into the Mainstream*. Tom was diagnosed with Parkinson's disease several years ago and now lives in residential care. He is no longer able to write, but his commitment to socialist ideas remains as strong as ever.

This new edition of *Rebel Women* is the second book in a project to publish new editions of all Tom O'Lincoln's major works, ensuring that they will be available in perpetuity through print-on-demand services. Interventions is proud to be able to make this contribution to supporting the continued availability of Tom's enduring contribution to socialist history and analysis.

Janey Stone, Interventions

Introduction to the third edition

> Don't be too polite, girls, don't be too polite,
> Show a little fight, girls, show a little fight.
> Don't be fearful of offending in case you get the sack
> Just recognise your value and we won't look back.[1]

A rallying call for the 1969 Equal Pay campaign, Glen Tomasetti's song spelt out the combativeness and determination many women brought to the fight for equality.

It's this spirit that has echoed throughout Australian women's working-class history, from the Parramatta female convict factory riots during the 1820s and 1830s to the successful November 2021 12-day strike of the predominantly female workforce at fashion giant Country Road's warehouse. Country Road workers certainly found out how true other words of the song are, in the lines:

> The people at the top rarely offer something more
> Unless the people underneath are walking out the door.

And this spirit of class struggle, of women fighting for their rights, informs this book, framed around two issues: why Marxists look to the working class; and why this history continues to be relevant. *Rebel Women* is a revolutionary Marxist account of some key moments in Australian working-class history. The book covers campaigns and industrial action during the Depression, World War II and the postwar boom times, through to the 1980s and the disastrous Accord years. It presents case studies of four key industrial disputes. We see women workers standing up for their rights, whether for equal pay, against exploitative bosses, demanding decent wages and conditions, taking on the government or in solidarity with other workers. The chapters explore how workers – both women and men – can change their ideas, build solidarity against division and even go so far as to demand a fundamental change to the system. In the 1986 Victorian nurses' dispute, for example, the *Melbourne Sun* described the striking nurses as 'Irene Bolger's Nurses Liberation Front'.[2]

In her original introduction, Sandra Bloodworth noted that seeing women through a feminist framework leads to a picture of everlasting conflict between women and men and the idea that class struggle is 'male' and women's struggle is 'feminist'. Feminist historians such as Marilyn Lake have attempted to develop a feminist version of Australian history. Sandra points out:

> Such an analysis sits uneasily with the bitter class struggles of that period [1890s, early 1900s] and later. The women and men in the events included in this book...fought what they saw as attacks from an exploiting class of employers. Their greatest successes in gaining better living standards and in challenging sexist stereotypes concerning women were when they achieved high levels of class-consciousness and unity.

Why do we feel the need to continue to refer to the struggles in this book? Why do we think it important to keep them in print? Decades after the strikes and industrial action related here, it is clear that the stories still reverberate today; they need to be remembered, not as blueprints, but as lessons and inspiration for the future.

For two contemporary young left-wing women, the 1981 strike at the Kortex textile factory in Brunswick is a flashpoint. *Rebel Women* was the first book Kath Larkin, a campus activist and later trade union militant on the Victorian railways, read when she became involved in socialist politics. The chapter on the Kortex strike made a particularly strong impact on later readers. Belle Gibson, as a design student at RMIT's Brunswick campus forty years later, wanted to reveal the radical history of Brunswick and its textile industry for a student publication:

> The women of the Kortex factory or the workers at the Brickworks are basically written out of Brunswick's creative history. But I think they capture the grit, texture and creativity of Brunswick perfectly.[3]

The chapter on the Kortex strike shows how victory in the dispute came only after a determined struggle. Every day, the women met at the front of the factory to discuss the plans for that day, then stood on the picket line holding up placards with their demands. Although they faced anti-union thugs and police, the women gained confidence as the strike went on, becoming more certain that they could win. As they turned the trucks away and persuaded the few scabs to join them, workers from other textile factories also joined, and their strength grew.

Bahriye Akalin, one of the participants, looked back at her experience in 2020. In an interview, she talked about how, having learned to speak up for herself and to demand what was rightfully hers, she was able to stand up for her rights at work. She felt proud. That spurred her on to be more involved in other strikes and street mobilisation protests in the following years. She spoke encouragingly: 'Today's young people should fight for their rights – they will win every time'.[4]

Strikes can illustrate how women's oppression and their exploitation as workers combine and interact. Industrial action at work can spill over into family life, challenging racist and sexist stereotypes and building working-class consciousness and confidence. That was certainly the case at Kortex. Many workers there had family members working at Ford, Rowntree and other factories in the area, all of which had recently won a $25 wage rise through workplace actions. Inspired by these victories, the Kortex women learned important lessons in organising and were encouraged and supported by family members who'd been involved in their own actions.

Another crucial factor in the strikers' resolve was the presence of left-wing and socialist activists. The Victorian Turkish Workers Association (VTEB) and members of a small socialist organisation, the International Socialists (IS), played important roles in supporting the strikers and, in the case of VTEB, provided an alternative political leadership to the conservative union officials.

The campaign for equal pay in the insurance industry drew out some of the same lessons: the need for unity, militancy and a left-wing rank and file leadership able to defy the union officials if necessary. In the lead up to the dispute, social factors, including women's increased participation in the workforce and a younger, more proletarianised white-collar sector, fuelled a growing class-consciousness and combativeness. The rising Women's Liberation Movement made equal pay one of its key demands, and activists supported striking Sportsgirl machinists and women fighting for jobs as drivers in the tramways.

Diane Fieldes' chapter shows how the issue of equal pay drove insurance workers, female and male, to overwhelmingly support a national strike.

The fight for it showed how a common class interest could begin to bridge sexist divisions among workers. In the course of the campaign, workers of both sexes attended meetings in their thousands, banned overtime, marched in the streets and demonstrated outside insurance companies. The driving force was the union rank and file. The union, whose members had never struck before, gained hundreds of new members, and the campaign created a new attitude to women workers.

Historians have often portrayed women as passive or invisible in the class struggle, while accusing unions and the left, primarily the CPA, of being dismissive or even hostile to women's demands. In fact, it has often been feminist historians who have written out women's militant history, or ruling class women who have actively tried to suppress working women's fight for their rights. In the end, class has been the determining factor in the history of women's struggle in Australia. Janey concludes:

> [e]ven a 'national cause' as intense as the war could not abolish the class divisions affecting both genders. As working women faced new difficulties in the postwar era, a class conflict would again shape their lives.

The chapters by Janey Stone and Tom O'Lincoln illustrate this. Throughout the 1930s and 1940s, working-class women were often in the thick of the fight – as workers themselves, in militant women's committees in the waterfront, mining and manufacturing unions, or in social movements. One woman reminisced:

> we were always fighting and demonstrating in those days. It made me a militant...you had to get into the struggle to survive...we were all in it together...although we had nothing...you didn't have time to think of your own troubles.

The Communist Party, by the 1940s thoroughly Stalinised, often had a more contradictory position on women. Tom O'Lincoln described its attempts to keep women at work 'for the war effort'; however, it also encouraged women workers' activism, both inside and outside unions, around equal pay and issues such as child care, inflation and housing. It also kept the working-class history and aims of International Women's Day (IWD) alive.

Bookending *Rebel Women* are two chapters that challenge the stereotypes of women. Beginning the book, Sandra Bloodworth's chapter on the women in the mining town of Broken Hill uncovers the hidden history of women's participation in the 1890s and the 1909 miners' strike and lockout, through to anti-conscription campaigns and more. Women played an active role on the picket lines, with large numbers confronting scabs and joining marches, rallies and mass meetings. There was constant political debate around the role of women, class struggle and socialism during these times; again, it was the militant socialists and unionists who carried the arguments for equality, for a new world.

Finishing the book is my chapter on the 1986 Victorian nurses' strike. Nursing was seen as a stereotypical women's job, one that would prepare them for marriage and children. It was a job centred on dedication, not workers' rights. But, over the years, nurses began to challenge these notions, displaying banners such as 'Dedication doesn't pay the rent' prominently during a growing number of campaigns and industrial actions. In the 1986 strike, nurses found their strength. One commented: 'For the first time, thousands of nurses here are finding that they do have power, that they can change their own lives.'[5] Led by a rank and file strike committee, including some socialists, the strike inspired other workers and put another nail in the coffin of the myth of women's passivity. After a series of defeats in other arenas, it showed how workers could win, even during the class collaborationist years of the ALP–ACTU Accord.[6]

As this new edition of *Rebel Women* is published, in the midst of a Covid pandemic, the lessons of the struggles it describes continue to echo. In 2021, for example, the mostly female workforce at Country Road stood up against an intransigent management that was determined to deny them fair wages and conditions. While offering a pittance to workers, with scant regard for their health during the pandemic, the company increased its profits by 44 percent and took $25 million in government Jobkeeper payments – actually designed to benefit struggling firms, not fashion mega-houses.

Meanwhile, workers deemed 'essential' under the Covid protocols risked their lives daily with insufficient protection in the warehouse – forced to take breaks in outside tents with no heating, no cooling and no airflow.

Although they initially lacked confidence, both female and male workers found that the experience of the strike and picket quickly changed them. One described how the strike 'united us…the union has given us backbone to feel united and stand up for each other…we're feeling very confident and very brave.'[7] Impressively, at a time of few working-class victories and during a pandemic, the workers won most of their demands.

Rebel Women plays an important role in recovering women's working-class history. That history demonstrates that the working class, united in its struggles against capitalism, is key to winning a truly liberated society. Spanning nearly 100 years in Australian history, this book remains an inspiration for those wanting both to understand history and to organise to build a better, socialist, future.

Liz Ross, Melbourne, 2022

Introduction to 1998 edition

If women's studies means the study of women 'objectively', that is, as though they were a species of ant, it doesn't matter which group of women we study. But if we are looking at history to analyse the world, in order to change it, then it matters very much.

Our starting point is an understanding that the world can be fundamentally changed, and women liberated, by the everyday struggles of working-class people. The articles collected here were all written to record the achievements of, and the lessons we can learn from, those struggles. They are particularly relevant today when all around we are faced with pessimism about the ability of ordinary people to change the world.

The contributors to this book are revolutionary Marxists. Our starting point is our conviction that the oppression of women is a source of disunity among workers. The experience of struggle offers the best opportunity to combat sexist ideas held by male workers, and for women to overcome the constraints on their involvement in political life, and therefore to forge unity. This is a theme in Marx's work which is rarely discussed in academic writing. In his *Theses on Feuerbach*, Marx considered the problem of how workers could change their ideas, given that they are conditioned by social circumstances. This could only occur in struggle; people would change themselves as they fought to change the world. 'The coincidence of the changing of circumstances and of human activity or self-change can be conceived and rationally understood only as revolutionary practice.'[1]

This is not an automatic process, which is why we have attempted over the years to record lessons and insights from the actual experiences of class conflict. The development of class-consciousness and opposition to divisive ideas such as sexism, often results from the initiatives and intervention of militants – both women and men – who have a political world view that says unity is necessary and possible, who consciously see the possibilities, and who are prepared to seize them. The dynamic of the struggle itself – a striving for unity, open conflict with figures of authority – can make workers more open to ideas which challenge the dominant 'common sense'. This is why the high points of struggle are of particular interest. In periods of 'normality', the divisive ideas in society are the most entrenched. If this is what we focus on, we miss the potential for change. This point is driven home by R. H. B. Kearns' pictorial history of Broken Hill. The book is dominated by photos and graphics of men. But the chapter 'The Miners' stands out, with illustrations of women in the struggles.[2]

In the late 1990s, this approach seems much more out of step with the latest thinking – both in the left of the labour movement and in academic circles – than it may have seemed in the 1970s. In the trade union movement, the experience of 13 unhappy years of Australian Labor Party (ALP) government – increased bureaucratisation of the unions, falling membership, to say nothing of cuts to the social wage, mass unemployment and attacks on the conditions of those who do work – demoralised a generation of militants who were convinced by both left-wing and right-wing officials and Labor Party politicians that class collaboration under the ALP-ACTU (Australian Council of Trade Unions) Accord was the modern, 'smart' way for unions to increase their influence. Since the election of the Howard government in 1996, we have seen the consequences of this strategy. The unions (and the left) have been incapable of leading a coordinated, sustained campaign against either Howard's attacks on union rights, welfare, migrants and Aboriginal and Torres Strait Islander people or (One Nation Party leader) Hanson's racism.

The academic world provided theoretical respectability to these ideas: the era of radicalism was (thankfully) over; the working class was no longer a central player in the struggle for social change, if ever it had been. Social movements, with their claim to provide cross-class alliances (as opposed to the alleged divisiveness of class struggle) were hailed in the early to mid-1980s as the road to social change. But, as the industrial struggle declined under the influence of the Accord and bureaucratic control from above, so did the social movements. Fashionable theories now turned against any genuinely left agenda. Theories of 'postmodernism', which rejected all attempts to understand the totality of society, no longer lingered in the shadows created by the growing disarray on the left. By the late 1980s, they were basking in the academic limelight, condemning and even ridiculing any attempt to find patterns in history from which we might learn for the future.

INTRODUCTION TO 1998 EDITION

Increasingly, history is viewed as mere 'myths' created by historians' own personal interpretation of events. The fragmentation of the left and working-class movement, rather than being studied as a problem to be overcome, was glorified with calls for 'identity' politics, whereby every oppressed group emphasised their 'difference' from, rather than solidarity with, others. 'Totalising' theories such as Marxism, which claimed to be able to make sense of the seeming chaos and fragmentation and which argued for a collective struggle of all the oppressed, based on the power of the working class, were increasingly dismissed as *totalitarian* – an argument which confused ideas and material power, but which nonetheless had an appeal in the prevailing climate of political confusion.

The studies in this book, undertaken in the contexts of both academic study and experience in the struggles themselves, illustrate our reply to the dominant pessimism and doubt about the ability of working-class people to change history. They show that history is not a chaotic, unpredictable jumble of events; rather, we can find common themes that point to ways to overcome sexism and women's oppression. And it is the struggles of workers themselves which reveal the pattern. For most of the time, it is true that capitalism so dominates our lives that all around seems madness and chaos. The market, said by economic rationalists to be the saviour of modern society, serves to mystify the processes by which society operates. Marx called this 'commodity fetishism'. He argued that, if the actual reality could be directly understood from the surface appearance of things, we would not need theory. But how are we to push aside the veil of mystification? This book illustrates Marx's argument. Practical experiences from the 1890s to the 1980s, and from remote Broken Hill to the heart of Melbourne, show that people's view of the world can be transformed in struggle.

My first chapter looks at the role women played in 1892–1917 in Broken Hill, a centre famous for its industrial struggles and dominated by the all-male unions in the mines. I also discuss some of the complexities in interpreting the records of such events. Janey Stone's account of women's militancy during the Depression is a direct reply to the idea that women have generally been passive, or simply dupes of men, in times of hardship and resistance. At times, women had to confront working-class men in order to be involved. They often were able to do this because of the political leadership of Communist Party women and the confidence arising from a climate of struggle. Their activity, as in Broken Hill, was made possible by their identification as working-class fighters with a common interest with the men.

These themes are continued in Janey Stone's account of events during World War II, when the key issue was equal pay. She shows how women could be more militant than men, despite immense pressures on them to conform to feminine stereotypes, and that women fought on both sides of the class divide. Tom O'Lincoln highlights a different aspect of women's involvement by looking at the role women played in the CPA. He demonstrates our point in the negative. When the level of class struggle was at a very low level, as it was during the Cold War, there were very few gains for women's rights. Diane Fieldes' article on the campaign for equal pay in the insurance industry highlights the fundamental importance of class divisions, rather than gender – even on this issue, which is sometimes assumed to have received little support from male workers. She shows that the struggle for equal pay 'pitted class against class' and 'illustrated how a common class interest could begin to bridge sexist divisions among workers themselves.' Women in management positions, by and large, sided with their cohorts in opposition to equal pay, while men in the lower ranks of the workforce could be won to support it.

The last two chapters are accounts of strikes by women workers in the 1980s, written on the basis of the authors' direct involvement. Liz Ross' account of the 1986 nurses' strike in Victoria illustrates the dynamic of class solidarity, which can override sexist attitudes among male workers when women break out of the stereotypes. My account of the Kortex strike in 1981 draws out the impact of class struggle on forging solidarity, on combating bosses and officials, and on relationships in the home as well as the workplace.

The details of the militancy of women in these struggles are drawn largely from primary sources. Many of the facts about strikes, political activity or women's support for male trade unionists' struggles had not been published before these articles were written. To unearth this history, and keep it alive, is a continual struggle.

In Broken Hill, for example, there is a folk history of the women's sometimes riotous activities which is a source of pride for Broken Hill workers.[3] It is portrayed in the painting 'United We Stand', by Howard William Steer and Clark Barrett, that sometimes hangs in pride of place as you enter the City Art Gallery. As miners hold the police at bay, women are tarring and feathering scabs. A mural on a wall down the street features women and children rallying with their banners. Yet, this folk history has to be reasserted continually to survive. The Tourist Centre in the town features a large display about past union struggles which does not include even one of the many available illustrations of women's involvement.

Why have labour historians so often ignored the sorts of struggles discussed here? To some extent, this can probably be put down to the general gender blindness of much social science. That, however, is not sufficient explanation.

Much of labour history tends to emphasise the official structures of trade unions and the Labor Party. Because of their oppression, women are less likely to be represented in these structures.

In Broken Hill, in the coal mining areas and in the metals industry, this is exaggerated even further because of the overwhelmingly all-male membership of the unions. Moreover, because they are not workers, rather occupying a position as brokers between capital and labour, union and ALP officials tend to be more conservative, more concerned to be 'respectable' than their rank and file, especially in times of struggle.[4] This conservatism among full-time officials is evident in many of the struggles recounted here.

However, when we focus, as this book does, on the activities of the rank and file, the political life of women (and men not in the leadership) takes on much greater significance.

The two photos of a speech by Tom Mann at Broken Hill illustrate the point. The one that centres our attention on the speaker, a picture that has become famous, creates the impression that the workers' movement can be represented by the images of individuals, generally men. When the camera directs our view at the crowd, however, the movement is seen as a collective, and the anonymous crowd comes alive. Women are in the minority, but they are now visible as part of the movement. But this view has been left unnoticed in the archives.

Similarly, Diane Fieldes' chapter on the fight for equal pay in the insurance industry draws out how important it is to differentiate between the attitudes of the union officials and the potential militancy of the rank and file: even initially quite conservative workers would respond well to coherent arguments for struggle. Male members the officials had written off as sexist proved able to outgrow their conservative ideas as the campaign unfolded.

At high points in struggle, there is a tendency for rank and file militants of any gender to challenge the union officials and burst out of the constraints of everyday trade unionism. Often, it is women who prove the more radical in such situations, as many of our chapters demonstrate. This arises, ironically, from the very fact that, in 'normal' times, they are less likely to be involved in trade union affairs. As a result, they are less prey to conservative traditions. Historical accounts focusing more on the labour movement's institutions and less on the high points of struggle tend to miss this fact and, therefore, dismiss women as backward elements.

If traditional history has neglected these aspects of working class experience, however, attempts by feminist historians to write 'women's history' have not redressed the omissions. This is not simply a question of empirical research. In the

Tom Mann addressing street meeting in Broken Hill. The view from the stage (below) reveals many women in the audience.

first burst of the Women's Liberation Movement, attempts were made to unearth the side of women's history which challenged the idea that they have been implacably passive in the face of struggle; that their role has been solely rooted in the home. This was not, however, a majority stance even then. Janey's chapters were written explicitly as a refutation of the idea carried even by feminists that women were, by and large, passive in the class struggle. Liz Ross and I thought it necessary to explicitly draw out how our account was a refutation of such a position.

From the beginning, the idea that there is some common interest between all women blurred the class divisions between them. Janey showed how both upper-class and working-class women could be militant, on different sides of the barricades. It was not enough to simply laud their actions. She drew out the reactionary nature of the former and the progressive dynamic of workers' struggle. And she pointed out that the assumption that their oppression meant that women could not be independent agents of history distorted the conclusions of feminist historians:

> Carmel Shute, in her study of the propaganda of the conscription struggle during World War I, in spite of having shown the militancy and level of independent organisation of women on both sides of the struggle, concludes that 'women were a tool to be used by men, both by concrete and on an ideological level.'[5]

However, as feminist historiography has grown and developed, there has emerged another, more important barrier to historians' taking an interest in the struggles of working-class women such as those in this book. It is associated with the decline of the mass movements. As the optimism and radicalism of the 1970s gave way to pessimism and doubts about the validity of class struggle, confusion over what, exactly, is 'labour history'[6] gave rise to scepticism about the value of a history of women in working-class struggle. The demand that 'gender become a central category of all historical analysis' has increasingly become the basis for a polemic against 'class analysis' and the identification of class struggle as 'the struggle between men for domination.'[7]

This is not simply a theoretical debating point. A history of 'women' necessarily emphasises what all women have in common: their oppression. In the early 1970s, feminist writers hoped that focusing on those aspects of life which are specific to women – such as children, women's sexuality and housework – could radically change widely-held ideas about history. Writing history from the point of view of the oppressed (women) instead of the oppressors (men) would enable a whole new historiography to emerge. It has. However, whole aspects of women's histories do not fit this framework – and so have continued to be ignored.

The emphasis on oppression, and the aspects of life all women share, at least in the stereotypical view of women, blurs the enormous class differences of this experience. So the fact that a struggle around economic issues could lead women to become involved in activities which broke down these stereotypes, or the fact that a women's fight for a pay rise could lead men to take on home duties and child care, are unrecognised. The fact that it was by picketing, defying the Accord and resisting police attacks that nurses won respect instead of wolf whistles from male workers such as the Builders' Labourers' Federation (BLF) is unlikely to be noticed. The experience of the insurance industry campaign, where getting female *and* male members involved was so important in building a mass campaign – a move initially resisted by the union officials – will probably be ignored or played down.

Moreover, focusing on what all women have in common can mean implicitly reintroducing the oppressive stereotypes which led to the desire for women's liberation in the first place. Women begin to be seen primarily as victims; their suffering becomes central to their history, regardless of whether they resisted, whether they lived out the stereotypes or not. Janey put it clearly:

> In this way, the emphasis on women's specific oppression is quite one-sided. It refixes women firmly back into the oppressive passivity of their role, with no way to escape. It accepts that the role as prescribed is the same as the reality. The officially-accepted female role is returned to us gift-wrapped by the new feminist historians.[8]

These trends virtually guarantee that working-class women's role in the class struggle will remain unrecognised or misrepresented, even when they are the subject of history. Joy Damousi, a Melbourne historian, has summed up many of the arguments. Her conclusions are particularly relevant because she has looked at women activists in working-class organisations. An example from her book *Women Come Rally* illustrates the problem. In December 1906, two socialist activists from Melbourne, Lizzie Ahern and Mrs Anderson, visited Broken Hill as representatives of a free speech campaign in Melbourne. At their reception, the Labor mayor, Alderman Ivey, said that their names 'would be recorded in history' because they had been jailed 'for preaching the gospel of Socialism.'[9] It is not accidental that, contrary to Alderman Ivey's expectation, and after promising to 'respect...the historical actors within the context and milieu of their times', Damousi says Lizzie Ahern was 'inspired by a desire to further the cause of women.'[10] This is far too one sided.

Ahern shared other socialists' attitude that the fight for socialism was just as relevant for women as men because it was only under socialism that women would not be oppressed. When Ahern married, she entered her occupation on the marriage certificate as 'Socialist agitator'.[11] This is one small point, but it indicates a wider problem. The identification of class struggle as 'male' is so well established in feminist historiography that it is, to a large extent, taken for granted. Damousi claims that 'class solidarity is linked with masculinity and "class unity" becomes the prerogative of male workers'.[12] But, for activists such as Lizzie Ahern, their whole emphasis was on class struggle and working class unity. Damousi emphasises one aspect of Ahern's activism (campaigning for women's rights) which implies that she was a feminist – when she was known as, and identified herself as, a socialist.

Marilyn Lake, a well-known feminist historian who began her career as a labour historian, has developed the argument in a different direction, arguing that:

> one of the greatest political struggles in Australian history [was] the contest between men and women at the end of the nineteenth century for the control of the national culture'[13]

This argument was repeated and developed in *Creating a Nation*, the feminist reinterpretation of Australia's history which has become standard reading for many university courses. The authors effectively subsumed working-class

Women in May Day parade Sydney 1933

women's history into that of the middle-class feminist movements and identified the class battle as male.[14] These two forces, they contend, fought for domination of Australia during the 1890s and the early 20th century, ending with a 'feminisation' of Australia which men bitterly resisted. Such an analysis sits uneasily with the bitter class struggles of that period and later. The women and men in the events included in this book – Broken Hill until 1917, in the factories and on the coalfields of the 1930s, in the munitions and textile factories during World War II, demanding equal pay in the insurance industry in the seventies, plus migrant textile workers and nurses defying all odds for a pay rise in the eighties – fought what they saw as attacks from an exploiting class of employers. Their greatest successes in gaining better living standards and in challenging sexist stereotypes concerning women were when they achieved high levels of class-consciousness and unity.

The stories in the chapters that follow are often exciting in their own right. But it is not simply a question of 'adding on' this women's history to that of so-called 'male' stories – a fear of feminists since the 1970s. The fact that historians have obscured the women merely makes their account of history 'masculinist', not the events themselves. The very fact of solidarity between working-class women and men contradicts the notion that class struggle is 'male' and women's struggle is 'feminist'. The fact of women's activity which defied the stereotypes expected of them points to ways in which lasting gains could be won. In these times of declining union membership and historically very low levels of industrial disputation, Diane's article is a timely reminder. She found that, as industrial action picked up, workers joined the union in increasing numbers. So these women's histories change the whole concept of what has been possible and what will be in the future – essential insights for anyone who wants not just to analyse and describe the world, but to change it.

The way history is written and interpreted can make a significant difference to the way workers respond to the problems we face today. For example, the common feminist argument that militant class struggle is 'male' leaves the most conservative sections of the workers' movement unchallenged. Marilyn Lake, like many influenced by the Women's Liberation Movement in the seventies, had once been stirred by 'that exciting, idealistic and inspiring story that linked past dreams to present-day struggles'. Yet, today, she applauds arguments by conservative union leaders that downplay the importance of struggle: 'Unions now offer women "care", "protection", "friendship", and a "voice"... Strikes are presented as a "last resort". This supposedly 'fresh iconography' which 'substitutes the values of friendship for power'[15] is really only a new packaging of conservative labourism which has been with us since the beginning of trade unionism. This is precisely the mentality that led union officials to resist demands for militant struggle around equal pay during World War II, and again during the 1974 insurance industry campaign.

This representation of 'gendered subjectivity' leaves intact the stereotypical image of women as less aggressive than men, reluctant to participate in militant political action and struggle. And, indeed, 'one can only hope that none of the feminist workers has to face a recalcitrant employer'.[16]

The struggles in this book were not part of a generalised, revolutionary struggle to transform the whole of society. Nonetheless, they reveal the potential for unity between male and female workers and the possibilities for struggle to begin to challenge the oppressive roles which are central to women's oppression. They also reveal the unbridgeable gulf between working women and the women of the capitalist class, against which workers must struggle for every improvement in their lives. They show how women can emerge as leaders of strikes and campaigns. Finally, they demonstrate the possibilities for overcoming, in the course of the fight, sexist prejudices among their male workmates.

Such lessons are forgotten or ignored in much feminist writing today. But they leap out at us from the history of these rebel women.

Sandra Bloodworth

THIS MEMORIAL IS DEDICATED TO THE WOMEN OF BROKEN HILL WHO HAVE STOOD BY THEIR MEN DURING TROUBLED INDUSTRIAL TIMES

Militant spirits
The rebel women of Broken Hill

SANDRA BLOODWORTH

A beautiful day in August 1892 became known in Broken Hill as the Fateful 25th. By mass picketing, striking workers and their supporters prevented the mine owners from reopening the mines with blacklegs. This victory owed much to the enthusiasm and militancy of women on the pickets, who, armed with axe and broom handles, led foray after foray against blacklegs and shift bosses with vigorous violence. To the horror of conservative opinion, the 'inevitable women' molested a respectable businessman and seized the reins of a bank manager who rode his horse into the crowd. Popular legend has it that they also tarred and feathered scabs.

The degree to which the success of the day was attributed to the women can be judged by this sour comment in the mouthpiece of conservative opinion on the Barrier, the *Silver Age*:

> It would be a grave error for the leaders to assume that because a crowd of men did not face the tar pots and the viragos yesterday morning the victory is theirs.[1]

The unionists had been on strike since 4 July against the introduction of stoping (excavation) by contract. The workers firmly believed that this was a cover for a wage cut and would result in more dangerous work practices.

On Sunday 3 July, 5,000 people, including a good number of women, gathered in the treeless Central Reserve. It was agreed that only unionists could decide on a strike motion. They would ultimately be held responsible for the suffering endured by families and others in the town. But Josiah Thomas, mindful of the potential strength of a union which involved its supporters, both women and men, put forward another motion. In part, it read: 'as the Miners' Association is the most chiefly concerned, this meeting supports any action the miners may think fit, whether immediate or otherwise.' The speeches emphasised the common interest of the miners, other unionists and women and families. Thomas' motion was carried unanimously, cementing a sense of solidarity and determination which was to ensure a wide involvement and keep the strike going until 23 October.[2]

Many women regularly attended the daily mass rallies and pickets. In the first weeks of the struggle, a Barrier United Females' Strike Protest Committee formed. The assembly of 500 passed a large number of resolutions, one of which was to join the union demonstration planned for 24 August. This idea was wisely, in the view of the *Barrier Miner*, abandoned.[3] Nevertheless, plans were made for a women's rally which, some said, was the highlight of the Fateful 25th, in spite of the excitement of the morning. In any case, a contingent of about 100 women did join the union procession and was favoured with a perfect volley of claps and applausive shouts.

Five hundred marched later in the women's procession, a bold and daring activity for the times. Three times that number lined the streets to support them. Mrs C. Poole, mounted on a handsome bay, acted as field marshal.

Even the *Silver Age*, a hostile judge, admitted that 'several of the ladies present…discoursed eloquently and intelligently upon the situation at their rally.' Thousands had gathered in the Central Reserve to support the women's march. Mesdames Rogers, Hastings, McDonald and Trevarrow, along with Miss Roberts, were hoisted onto a lorry and: 'delivered short addresses condemnatory of the directors' action and the contract system… They heartily prayed that the men would stand firm.'

Mrs Rogers threatened a man who attended the last women's meeting dressed in women's clothing: 'if the women caught him there again, they would see if they could make a woman of him.'[4]

Large and enthusiastic meetings of women continued even after some militants thought that the strike was defeated; seven of the strike leaders had been jailed, and hundreds of scabs were working. Women crowded the streets for the annual Eight Hours Day procession. Some who claimed to have taken blacklegs out of the mine rode on a vehicle displaying a banner emblazoned: 'Women's Union'. They were involved in riotous scenes confronting scabs on Saturday nights.

Mary Lee, Vice-president of the Working Women's Trades Union, Adelaide, wrote to the *Barrier Miner*:

Sir, this strike has one feature which renders it more profoundly interesting than any of its predecessors...which must secure it a prominent and distinguished page when the history of these colonies shall be written. It is that the women of Broken Hill are the first great body of working women who have raised their voices in united protest against the glaring injustice that 'the present constitution will not allow them a voice in framing the laws'[5]

She was right to give the strike such historical significance. But, for all the efforts to write a women's history in recent years, it has not received a distinguished page. It has not warranted one sentence. Even when working-class women's experience intersects with issues such as suffrage, it has escaped historians' notice.

This kind of political and militant activity seems extreme and unusual. However, it was part of a recurring pattern in Broken Hill. Three years earlier, a Women's Brigade picketed the mines, during a week-long strike to establish compulsory unionism for the all-male workforce, and tarred and feathered scabs.

The next great confrontation, the 1909 lockout, saw women mobilise again.

Crowd in the street after a procession during 1909 lockout

1909 women's strike relief committee

Broken Hill was in ferment in the last months of 1908. The companies had summarily dismissed demands for a wage increase and shorter hours, and BHP was even threatening a pay cut. The *Barrier Truth* Women's League, set up by the union paper, was involved in organising, propagandising and agitating, preparing women for the expected showdown. But they were not left to do it alone. On the afternoon of Wednesday 14 October and again on Monday 19 October, Tom Mann, the famous and much loved union organiser recently employed by the Barrier unions, addressed the League at Trades Hall.

The Wednesday meeting resolved to stand with the men and to help them by all means in their power, not just because of loyalty to their men, but to resist any lowering of the standard of living on the Barrier. In fact, they were more demanding than the unionists, who were prepared to continue with the old agreement: 'We call upon the men to claim the half-holiday as a reasonable concession.'[6] They set up a strike committee and resolved to meet weekly. The new Lady Editor of the 'Women's Sphere' column in the *Barrier Truth* promised to deal chiefly with issues that affected the economic interest of working-class women. The women asked the Combined Trade Unions to produce a badge, to be worn by both sexes; if unionists were seen without it, committee women would have the right to challenge them. Lizzie Ahern, a popular speaker from the Victorian Socialist Party now living on the Barrier, gave talks such as 'The War of the Classes'.

After more than a decade of relative peace, the Women's League had only 21 members. But they were to mobilise thousands in the months to come. Their task as militants was organising more women into the struggle, but this was not solely their responsibility. Nor did they attend only women's meetings. The Lady Editor used her column to call on women to swell the meetings. Tom Mann, in his address at Trades Hall on 'The Social Upheaval: Its Causes and Cure', urged the women to use their influence to get the men into the union.[7]

The picketing began on Friday 1 January. A marked feature of the previous Wednesday's mass meeting was the large number of women present who held their hands up conspicuously when the vote was taken. From the beginning, women were on the pickets. An extraordinarily large number of women were seen at the rallies, which heralded shift changes every four hours. Lizzie Ahern, now known as Mrs A. K. Wallace (since her wedding on 10 December), addressed a monster crowd and urged all to stand firm in the fight they had undertaken. Sometimes, they could be relentless in their demand for solidarity. L. E., in Women's Sphere, pointed out that it was good that Tom Mann appealed to the women and got a positive response. But the Tramways delegate at the same meeting had made a:

> knock kneed, apologetic speech about why his union could not stop provisions getting into the scabs in the mine. There is only one place for him – on the other side.[8]

At a mass meeting on Friday 8 January, Tom Mann asked how many of the women present would march at the head of the union procession the next day – quite a new departure, as the *Barrier Daily Truth* put it. They responded enthusiastically. Thirty males (and no females) were arrested that day. Being female might save women from custody, but it did not shield them from the baton blows.[9]

Women played their part in isolating police brought in from Sydney. After the police attack on 9 January, women responded that night with backhanders and by spitting at police. On a Saturday night, one girl ignored a policeman's order to 'come here', throwing back the remark: 'Go back to Sussex St, you plague rat'. And the police were later to allege that Mrs Gibson, one of the leading lady socialists, used insulting words for which she spent one month in jail.[10]

The incarceration of unionists and Mrs Gibson provided another reason for frequent demonstrations. A Mrs Nolan was the flag bearer for the Socialist Group. At the court, she defiantly waved the red flag over the fence, and her action was loudly cheered. Mrs Wallace spoke, condemning the police as scabs and castigating men who stood on the footpaths instead of joining the marches. She pointed out that the capitalists raised the old cry of women's suffering in the struggle; but the suffering would not be half so great as if their husbands and fathers accepted lower wages.[11] Her point was driven home by the ambiguous result, which left hundreds of men unemployed for months after the lockout was called off on 23 May. BHP defied the Arbitration Court's ruling in favour of the union by keeping the mine closed.

This legacy of industrial militancy helps to explain why Broken Hill saw the first strike against conscription during World War I. When Prime Minister Billy Hughes announced a referendum to introduce conscription, the militants sprang into action, reviving some of the old traditions and mobilising large numbers by linking anger about falling living standards and the desire for shorter hours with hostility to conscription.

The Barrier anti-conscription campaign opened in the Central Reserve on Sunday 16 July 1916. One week later, a mass meeting of 500 men and 'several staunch labor [sic] women' at Trades Hall formed the Labour Volunteer Army (LVA). Hundreds took an oath to the 'working class of Australia' not to 'serve as a conscript (industrial or military)…even though it may mean my imprisonment or death.'[12]

1889 Barrier United Females Strike Protest Committee

Cartoon depiction of women assaulting strikebreakers

The LVA Women's Corps received a boost with a three-week visit by Mrs Bella Lavender, the popular agitator from Melbourne. Promoted as one of the 'most intellectual women in the Commonwealth...the first of her sex in Australia to take the MA degree,'[13] Lavender spoke to large crowds on 'Australia's Peril' (the employing class), the 'War Precautions Act' and 'Man's Love for Woman' – in which she dealt with the status of women, industrially and socially.

The Corps held regular meetings at Trades Hall, had their own banners and formed their own choir which led their contingent in demonstrations. However, public speaking was still an area they found more difficult than men did, although many who took on the role of orators received a tumultuous welcome. Mrs Frances Mortimer, who told LVA rallies that workers must make war on war, wrote to a friend that she was the 'only woman in the Town who can get on the soapbox', adding: 'but the crowds like me.'[14] Adela Pankhurst, the famous suffragette from Britain, was a popular visiting speaker. There was such a crowd to hear her speak on 'War and the Workers' that she had to address an overflow meeting outside Trades Hall after the main event.

A number of male anti-conscription leaders received jail sentences. Typically, the police did not think women important enough to arrest. However, many lived with harassment; they had their mail opened and their activities kept un der constant surveillance.[15] Frances Mortimer lost her job as a result of a campaign by the secretary of the Jockey Club. The miners' union organised such an effective ban against the club that he, in his turn, was forced to resign and leave Broken Hill.

The second conscription referendum provoked similar activities. The frequent visits by women agitators – this time including Labor activist Kathleen Hotson – and the prominent role of women such as Mesdames M. Lawson, A. Barbor, Weaver, Sinclair, Joyce, Davis and Lumson had raised the expectations of larger numbers of women. They set up a speakers' class and asked Alice Cogan to coach them.

Workers took pride in the overwhelming rejection of conscription on the Barrier: 3,854 YES, 8,922 NO, with the no vote even larger in the second referendum of November 1917.[16]

Socialist Mrs Gibson, who spent a month in gaol for using insulting words to police

> # MISS ADELA PANKHURST
> WILL DELIVER A LECTURE ON
> ## "Women and War."
> IN THE TRADES HALL, IN THE TRADES HALL,
> WEDNESDAY NIGHT, at 8 O'clock.
>
> UNDER THE AUSPICES OF THE BARRIER LABOR FEDERATION.
>
> DON'T MISS YOUR LAST CHANCE TO HEAR
> MISS PANKHURST. MISS PANKHURST.
> ADMISSION: 6d.
> F. HYTTEN
> Secretary

Flyer advertising an appearance by famous British suffragette Adela Pankhurst

Ideas and the struggle for change

The following advertisement appeared in the first edition of the *Barrier Truth* in 1898[17] and was still running in 1917:

> A.M.A.
> The LEADING UNION of the BARRIER
>
> ---
>
> ALL THE WOMEN OF BROKEN HILL
> should persuade their HUSBANDS,
> FATHERS, BROTHERS, and all
> MALE RELATIONS to join, and
> should see that they KEEP
> GOOD ON THE BOOKS.
>
> ---
>
> IN CASE OF ACCIDENT
> the
> WOMEN AND CHILDREN
> REAP the BENEFIT.

It exemplifies the contradictions we need to keep in mind if we are to understand working-class history. By today's standards, the ad seems patronising; but there is another side to it. The union assumed that women read the union paper and were political. Therefore, they could be influenced; in turn, they could influence men and, thereby, play a role in building the union.

This tension between accepting gender stereotypes and treating women as political participants in working-class life was common in the language and rhetoric of socialists and militants. This is partly because all radicals operate within the historical and cultural restraints of their time. Early in that century, it was far more difficult to avoid childbirth and its consonant restraints. Child care was only for those who could pay a nanny. No family could afford to forgo a miner's pay for the low wages a woman could earn. This reality underpinned an acceptance of roles which are more open to challenge today.

In any case, even those prepared to challenge mainstream ideas do not always have clearly worked out alternatives. The very fact that socialists wanted to demonstrate their respect for women could lead them to emphasise the stereotypes: a responsible man gave his wages to his wife, that is, he was a reliable breadwinner, and she was faced with the task of making ends meet. A socialist might see some of the problems with this model and yet use its imagery to get a point across.

All radicals face this problem: how far can we be in advance of widely accepted ideas and still gain a hearing? The contradiction between ideas and activity can lead to confused rhetoric and representations which do not fully reflect the activity – or even to defensiveness in the face of an ideological offensive from their opponents.

These contradictions abounded in Broken Hill. The *Flame*, the local socialist paper, was notable for its hyperbole:

> It is difficult to rein one's self in at the thought of the indignities heaped upon brave women... And when it comes to gaoling a sensitive, high-souled publicist such as Tom Mann...to say nothing of the imprisonment barbarously inflicted upon bold men and good women, it is surely time that the liberty-loving people...rose to the occasion.[18]

Firstly, the women are brave, and the man is sensitive; then, the men are bold, and women are good. However, the left did consistently argue that women should be involved in the struggles of the working class. Thus, the *Barrier Truth* did not relegate their interests to one column. Items in the rest of the paper backed up the ideas of the Lady Editor and her contributors, emphasising both that socialism would mean social and economic emancipation for women and that they needed to join the fight.

The anniversary of the Paris Commune of 1871 was celebrated each year. It certainly was not portrayed as a celebration of male achievements, as is often claimed by feminist historians:

> What greater and grander sublimity can be depicted than that of men and women who are prepared to sacrifice their lives for even a dream?

The article emphasised female bravery: when soldiers tried to force Communards to kneel before their guns:

> one woman with a child in her arms refused to do so, shouting to her companions: 'Show these wretches that you know how to die upright'.

An article on the 1916 Dublin Uprising had a sub-header: 'The Bravery of the Dublin Girls'.[19] Tom Mann's speeches to the women's meetings were often about the role women were playing in international movements.[20]

Ambiguous rhetoric did not prevent women from building their own organisations and taking their own initiatives; nor did it prevent the unions from taking women and their activities seriously. In December 1906, the male trade unionists and the socialist mayor treated Lizzie Ahern and Mrs Anderson as respected activists when they visited Broken Hill to build support for a free speech campaign in Melbourne. Apart from a gruelling program of meetings, rallies and electioneering in searing heat, they visited the hospital, a source of both community pride and bitterness at government neglect, inspected the Stephens Creek reservoir and even went down a mine – the same tour given to male visitors.[21]

Miners' union secretary W. D. Barnett was responsible for authorising the notices in the *Barrier Truth* for the women's organising committee. This is not surprising, given the authority and power of the union. But, at times, he was also called upon to provide support in a less predictable manner. In 1908, the Lady Editor agitated for a 'monster meeting…when the situation can be fully talked over'. Women were to bring their neighbours and babies:

> Mr Barnett, our obliging secretary, will see they are looked after… Our men – God bless them– are fighting, but they don't mind minding babies whilst we confer.[22]

Conservative sections of the labour movement were more likely to portray the struggle in conventional terms. Claude Marquet's cartoon 'The Broken Hill Outrage', published by the Sydney *Worker*, is typical. On one side of the confrontation are businessmen, a policeman, and the vindictive daily press – represented by an old woman. On the other, the workers' struggle is epitomised by the clean-cut, brawny man, sheltering a frightened woman from the blows.[23]

For all the times men referred to women as mothers of the nation or talked of men's responsibility to defend them, there were other, genuine attempts to raise the rights of women. J. T. Kelly gave talks on birth control, the emancipation of women and their right to vote. Tom Mann argued for equal pay in his pamphlet *Socialism*. A conference held to form the One Big Union carried a motion that equal pay for the sexes be part of the objectives. Radical orators invariably referred to workers as men and women, as when Tom Barker, of the Industrial Workers of the World, told an anti-conscription rally that he: 'could see the time coming when men and women would conduct the economic affairs of the world on their own behalf.'[24]

However, the stereotypes of women provided a useful tool with which conservatives could attack militancy and sow divisions. In 1892, the *Silver Age* painted a lurid picture of the 'Amazon Brigade':

> **"THE WAR OF THE CLASSES."**
>
> **Stirring Address at the Hippodrome by a Lady Socialist.**
>
> Last night at the Hippodrome, Miss L. Ahern, member of the Victorian Sociaist Party, delivered an address on the subject: "The War of the Classes and its Settlement." Mr. R. S. Ross occupied the chair. There was a

Newspaper report of Lizzy Ahern's speech

Unemployed Union Women's Section

the females – they hardly deserve to be called women, were vowing vengeance, and that one woman related kicking in a hat with gusto...it can positively be said that but for them there would not have been the least interference with personal liberty.

The paper lectured the men about the 'extreme danger of allowing women of the class that were present interfering in their affairs', while asserting that most of the men 'rather resented the presence of these females'.[25]

Actually, in the march that followed, the women's contingent was cheered as it entered the Reserve. At the women's rally that afternoon, there were no recriminations. Thousands of unionists gathered to listen to the women orators. Only Richard Sleath, the union official, tried to restrain them; he:

urged the men to keep law and order... They did not want any disturbance, such as might be caused by a woman being roughly pushed or struck.[26]

The gender stereotype provided a useful ploy, but it cannot conceal the fact that the officials took steps to reduce the militancy of both males and females, not just on this day, but on a number of occasions when the rank and file wanted a tougher approach.[27]

Sometimes, the conservative papers drew on the stereotypes in attempts to make workers defensive about their actions. The *Silver Age* pontificated:

Cartoon depicting the leader of the Women's Brigade, which attacked strikebreakers in November 1889 with washing sticks, brooms and mops.

> We feel constrained to protest against the abortive attempt to drag from the seclusion of their homes the wives and mothers of the strikers... Surely we can fight an industrial war even to the bitter end without resorting to tactics worthy of Dahomey.[28]

At the height of women's involvement in the 1909 lockout, the conservative *Barrier Miner* used its occasional column 'Woman's World' to remind them that:

> it would be well for woman to remember that her special mission is to create a beautiful home life for her husband and family first, and then, if time allows, and her mental aspirations and ability go beyond that scope, she may seek to improve the social and moral conditions of less favoured humans.[29]

The marked difference in the response of the conservative papers and the *Flame* and the *Barrier Daily Truth* reflected class and political differences. This should serve to remind us of the danger in attributing sexist attitudes simply to the male sex in general.

Little can compare with the sexism of the police, who diligently kept watch on every activity and read every letter of both female and male activists during World War I. Alice Cogan and women with whom she corresponded were 'foolish women with crank social views'. But, because of her education and sincerity, Alice was 'capable of much harm among ignorant women and the children of Broken Hill.'[30]

Working-class militants saw capitalist sweat shops and recoiled, often vowing that women would not have to work under socialism. In the next breath, however, they could argue for women's economic independence. Sometimes, they argued against conscription on the grounds that men would be replaced by low-paid women, which would undercut living standards generally. But when M. A. Smedley argued that, if there was female labour, all they had to do was see that the women who replaced men got equal pay, he was applauded.[31]

Joy Damousi has argued:

> Prior to, and during the First World War, the public realm of speaking, proselytising and agitating was perceived to be the preserve of male activists. These activities were associated with manliness which found its expression in the public realm. Female activists were removed from their realm and occupied the domestic sphere.[32]

In fact, male activists in Broken Hill thought it essential for women to play a public role. The union paper expressed delight: 'A pleasing feature of the demonstration was the large number of enthusiastic women.'[33] Mick Considine, socialist President of the Amalgamated Miners' Association (AMA), considered it:

> a great pity for the industrial and political movement of the country that they did not have hundreds of women like Miss Pankhurst and Mrs Lavender.[34]

The opposition of private or domestic and public spheres is too often artificially used to impose a rigid division between women's and men's roles, thereby minimising the important role socialist women sometimes played. Joy Damousi takes the argument even further:

> Women's domestic work...[such as organising fundraisers, celebrations and concerts] not only circumscribed their contribution, it also was not considered to be political labour and thus devalued.

Therefore, she says, women were made responsible for Socialist Sunday Schools, seen as appropriate to their domestic role and considered lower in status than public tasks kept for the men.[35]

Yet, in Broken Hill, both women and men took responsibility for the Socialist Sunday School; they saw it as very important. When the Barrier Socialist Group wanted to start up a Sunday School, they invited Tom Mann to found it. It met in Trades Hall, which placed it firmly in the public life of the union movement. The school used a pamphlet called the *Lyceum Tutor* to educate the children on the role of women and men. Woman's 'natural position' was at the side of man, counselling in some things, being counselled in others; because, when circumstances are equal, woman has proved herself his equal. To the question: 'why should we give women other rights than those she has?' the *Tutor* answered: 'Justice asks it, and equity demands it. Woman has been wronged in the past and is entitled to reparation.' And, when she does the same work as man, she should be paid as he is.[36]

R. S. Ross, editor of the *Flame*, was superintendent, with one woman and five men as teachers in January 1908. In March, four women and four men taught the children. The school organised the Paris Commune celebration. In September, Mrs Glennie was secretary. The *Flame* proclaimed: 'we realise increasingly the

Eight Hours Day procession Broken Hill c. 1911

importance and responsibility of the Sunday School in relation to the Socialist cause, and indeed, the whole conduct of life.'

During the crisis from October 1908 into the lockout, the school was used to involve the children in the affairs of the unions. They sang a socialist hymn at Tom Mann's meeting.[37] Tom Mann addressed the scholars and advised them they were getting knowledge adults did not have, of poverty, capitalism and socialism.[38] A message from Percy Laidler, a prominent agitator and organiser, indicated that leading male socialists in other places were also closely associated with the schools' education: 'The scholars of the Melbourne Socialist Sunday School wish your fathers success in the fight.'[39] The children were expected to assemble on Sunday afternoon to assist with meetings held by the combined unions during the lockout.

Seven years later, the anti-conscription organisation, the LVA, had its own Sunday School. It was founded at a large meeting, on 5 November 1916, to which both sexes were invited. By 20 November, 103 children attended. Ern Wetherell, a well-known militant, was superintendent, assisted by Tom Hytten, Miss Alice Cogan and Mrs Bail. The children marched in anti-conscription rallies.

Women's Brigade assisting pickets during 1889 strike

Other areas of political work Damousi devalues are fundraising and organising cultural events and entertainment. She describes them as domestic or political work largely confined to private space and, therefore, relegated to women.[40] Because the rise of mass entertainment and the decline of the socialist movement have contributed to a separation of political events from entertainment, the latter seems of secondary importance today.

But this was not the case until at least the 1920s. All the industrial upheavals in Broken Hill to 1917 featured marches down city streets to the beat of the union band; rallies in the Central Reserve, at Trades Hall and on city corners; free concerts; and fundraising events. Political meetings often included a concert program of songs, poetry recitals, piano performances, skits and choirs. The work of organising and participating in such events was neither

seen as having a lower status than other political work nor regarded as solely women's responsibility.

In 1903, the Women's Political Association had a fundraising and social committee of both women and men who organised the AMA Band to play at their socials. Both women and men performed. The Socialist Group tried to set up a choir in 1906:

> By comparison with the effect of singing, the reading of the song we printed in last issue – 'The Red Flag' – is tame. We want to make the veins flow with melody, and the head swim with sound and revolt; and teaching the people the songs of humanity is the way to do it.[41]

A typical advertisement for a strike concert promised 'Sweet Song and Solid Education'. The songs would be rendered by 'Leading Lady and Gentlemen amateurs'.[42] During the 1909 lockout, a typical concert had nine male and six female performers.[43] In 1916, there were women and men on the LVA's social dance committee, and the strike concert in 1917 featured 13 men and six women. During the anti-conscription campaigns, Harry Kelly wheeled a piano around on a trolley to provide entertainment to all the demonstrations, rallies and mass meetings.

Just because historians often focus on orators and agitators, we should not assume that workers themselves saw the work of other activists as less political or less important. Workers had poor access to mass entertainment and only the

'Women protestors' wall mural in Broken Hill

most basic education from the state, so socialists took responsibility for providing both. If most women were not prominent as orators, neither were most men. Only a tiny minority of those who actively supported the aims of the unions were ever prominent in any of these ways.

Conclusions

Workers' ideas change in the course of struggle. The act of going on strike, of marching together down a street, has the potential to challenge both women's and men's deeply held ideas about appropriate behaviour. In the industrial and political struggles for which Broken Hill became famous, women's activity itself

helped to break down oppressive stereotypes. The need for solidarity led some men not just to accept this challenge grudgingly, but to encourage it. But this was not an automatic process. Socialists like Tom Mann argued at the height of the struggle for women's involvement, and the union paper commented on it and also helped to carry the arguments; these facts indicate that an ideological struggle had to take place. For this, there had to be militants who saw the need to challenge the ideas that divide workers. It was in the periods of struggle that their influence was most significant.

Why have labour historians not noticed this? Much of labour history tends to emphasise the official structures of the unions and the ALP. Because of their oppression, women are less likely to be represented in the official structures. They are more likely to be active at the rank and file level.

Much of the deconstruction of working-class history does little more than raise the obvious: women and men interpret their experiences, whether it be raising a family or organising a strike, through the prism of the dominant ideology. In Broken Hill, socialists confronted the reality of women and men's lives, organised around the gender stereotypes. During the period of this study, even the feminist movement accepted similar stereotypes. Images of women on their banners and publications are strikingly similar to the allegorical figures of trade union banners. Feminists emphasised the civilising, moderating influence women would have on political life if they were given the vote, and they invariably made their arguments in terms of women's mothering role.[44]

To concentrate on the gendered imagery, language and assumptions that permeate the working-class movement is to suggest that it is possible to overthrow the dominant ideas and culture of society without first destroying the social existence which gives rise to them. How this can be done is not clear, so the one-sided emphasis both reflects and entrenches the prevailing scepticism about class struggle.

Struggle is not sufficient to completely rework the language and iconography of a movement unless it brings about great changes in society. Socialists firmly believed that women would only throw off their oppression through the complete transformation of society – not an unreasonable assumption, given the problems we continue to experience despite the gains made for women's rights in recent times. If we focus too narrowly on the *forms* of their struggle, which were so greatly shaped by the limitations of their time, we miss the *content*, which challenged those limitations and which remains relevant today.[45] We fail to see the potential for women and men to challenge the dominant ideas of society and make a difference to the lives they lead.

George Dale's book *The Industrial History of Broken Hill* offers a testimony to the past and also a dialogue with the future. In his concluding pages, he sums up the importance of the history he recorded and which has been important for this chapter. It is fitting to conclude with his words:

> [W]e leave the destinies of this magnificent fighting industrial centre in the hands of the militant spirits of the present and future generations; and sincerely trust that some of the facts and phrases herein placed on record may prove beneficial to the coming agitator in the struggle for the emancipation of the working men and women.[46]

Wonthaggi miners and wives in 40 hour week demonstration in Melbourne 1930s

Brazen hussies and God's police
Fighting back in the Depression years

JANEY STONE

What took place during [the Depression] was a massive but mute mobilisation of Australia's housewives to fight for the survival of the institution which gave them their special role in society... In this way women helped ensure that even during a period of economic turmoil some basic form of social cohesion was maintained and that any threat of widespread revolt against the political and economic order which had caused the Depression was contained.

—Anne Summers, *Damned Whores and God's Police*[1]

The women however remain hidden in the background often in isolation... The sense of guilt and failure of unemployed women and of wives of the unemployed was no less strong, but it was internalised, was hidden from families, was brushed aside as unimportant in the face of the greater task of survival.

—Judy Mackinolty, *The Wasted Years*[2]

This is the conventional analysis of the Depression. Both writers criticise historians for paying less attention to women's suffering than that of men; both portray women as 'God's police', shoring up the collapsing social fabric. Margaret Power, likewise, argues that women 'served a valuable function in defusing discontent and maintaining social order.'[3]

Was that really the case? This chapter examines the 1930s and draws very different conclusions.

REBEL WOMEN

Cartoon about female hotel workers' action against police staying at coalfields hotels during 1929 lockout.

The economic background and the trade unions

Soon after the onset of the Depression, there was a 10 percent across-the-board wage cut, and many industries saw increased hours and eroded conditions. But, of course, the most pressing problem facing the working class was unemployment.

It is generally accepted that unemployment during the Depression was not as severe for women as for men. This was largely because they were restricted to certain sections of industry, which were not necessarily the worst hit. Twenty-five percent of breadwinners were women in 1933. Throughout the 1930s, the female workforce continued to grow, as did their labour force participation rate. However, the 1933 census showed 15 percent female unemployment (for men, it was 26 percent); and, because there must have been a great deal of hidden unemployment and underemployment, it is clear that conditions for women workers were harsh.[4]

Practically no relief work was available to them. Government sustenance was also denied. In 1932, Victorian Minister for Sustenance Kent-Hughes declared that, while domestic work was available at any wage, under any conditions, anywhere in the state, jobless women would be denied public assistance.[5]

The Depression is generally regarded as a time of unparalleled male chauvinism by male workers, because of the way male trade unionists attacked married women and blamed them for unemployment. It is certainly true that many trade unions were hostile to married women workers, and Queensland shop assistants actually had a parade of sandwich-board men as part of a campaign for legislation to exclude women from industry.[6] The Clothing Trades Union (CTU) seems to have had a policy, whether official or *de facto* is not clear, along the same lines.[7] Many other unions were similarly antagonistic. Muriel Heagney's disillusionment later on, in 1942, seems to anticipate a modern radical feminist perspective:

Frankly I have given up hope of achieving anything worthwhile immediately...the Labour Movement and the ACTU executive officers are so terribly reactionary in their views on women workers.[8]

Firstly, it must be said that the actual response was not entirely unmitigated sexism. While opposing married women, the CTU did give some help to young unemployed women and showed some concern by organising 'pound days' and collecting clothing. The union participated in a meeting of unemployed women at Trades Hall and gave financial help to individual members. Other unions helped in similar ways. In the late 1930s, at the instigation of Heagney, the unions founded the Council of Action for Equal Pay, which was active for several years.[9]

To fully understand the union officials' hostility, we have to see it in the context of a failure of the traditional methods of trade unionism: their customary approach could not cope with the problems posed by the Depression. It was not just misogyny, because the official trade unions failed male workers too.

Women's anti-scab march Port Adelaide 1939

BUT THEIR AUDIENCE WAS MOSTLY MEN

The Militant Women's Group held a rally in Belmore Park yesterday on behalf of the wives and families of the Timberworkers. They also launched a little gentle propaganda on behalf of their own organisation.

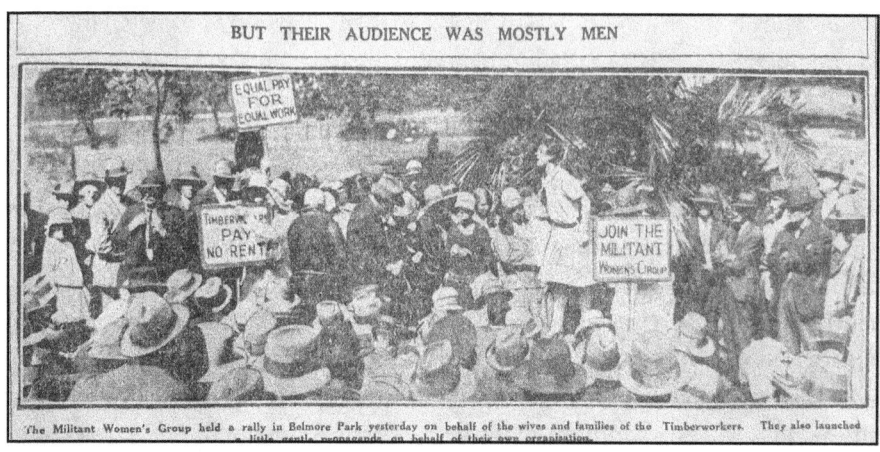

IWD rally organised by the Militant Women's Movement in support of striking timberworkers and wives, Sydney, 6 March 1929. Speaker Jean Thompson.

"A MILITANT WOMAN"

Prominent at the rally of the Militant Women's Group in Belmore Park yesterday—Miss Jean Thompson. She is typiste in Mr. Jock Garden's office.

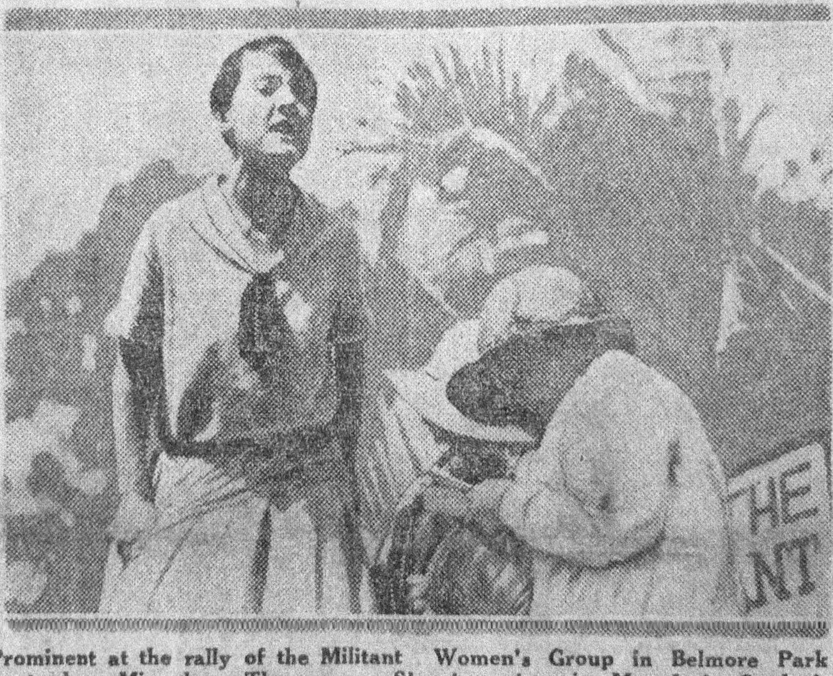

Militant Women's Movement publication *The Woman Worker* and membership card

Muriel Heagney late 1930s

The early Depression years were a time of working-class defeat. The economy began to slide towards depression and unemployment in 1927. From 1928, a series of major industrial confrontations initially involved the waterside workers, whose prolonged unofficial strike was broken, then major defeats of the timber workers and the miners on the northern New South Wales (NSW) coalfields. By the start of the Depression proper in 1929, many trade unionists were disillusioned with the failures of their existing leaders and were prepared to consider alternative and more radical ideas. This provided the Communist Party with opportunities, leading to the formation of the Minority Movement (MM) with its militant approach and attempt to raise consciousness on a range of issues.[10] It also provides the context for the rank and file actions that occurred sometimes independently of, and sometimes in opposition to, the union officials.

Let us look firstly at Heagney's approach in a little more detail.

The welfare approach

The assistance available to unemployed women was, admittedly, totally inadequate; but, even had the limited attempts been extended, and the full weight of the union movement been thrown behind Heagney's efforts, this would not have helped significantly to build a movement to liberate women. Heagney's approach was fundamentally flawed.

There is no doubt that women were worse off than men in some ways. The plight of unemployed single women who had no family to fall back on was desperate. In response to their predicament, Muriel Heagney organised a 'Girls' Week' in Melbourne in 1930, which raised £5,000. This money founded an Unemployed Girls' Relief Movement (UGRM) whose main activity was the establishment of centres where the 'girls' could drop in for company, use sewing machines or attend education courses. They also offered relief work, in cooperation with the government: in return for a small allowance, the women sewed clothes or made jam to be distributed to the needy. Large numbers of women passed through the doors of the centres, and Heagney believed that their effort 'in building up a women's cooperative movement...[was] without parallel in Australia.'[11]

A group of Sydney Labor women carried out a politically similar type of work; NSW Premier Jack Lang gave them the use of a building, which they ran as a hostel for homeless women without any further government assistance. Jessie Street – another well-known feminist of the time – and her United Associations of Women were also concerned to help the female unemployed. A meeting of women's organisations in 1931 decided on a strategy of teaching women to farm.[12]

Numerous other examples of voluntary relief work were generally consistent with what Summers calls the God's Police role. At the time, the communist newspaper *Working Woman* attacked these efforts, claiming that, in one of the sewing centres, material was cut into strips and then sewed together again just to keep members occupied.[13]

But criticism at this level is quite inadequate. Even if the participants had been very usefully employed, and even if the government had not interfered with their operation, there are serious problems with such a strategy. These centres were effectively a form of work for the dole. It might have been better than starvation, but they represented very cheap labour, severely undercutting women's already miserable wage rates.[14]

Summers herself accurately criticises the welfare approach of middle-class voluntary work:

> They unwittingly collaborated in the perpetuation of these injustices by devoting their energies to trying to alleviate the symptoms of that distress, rather than fighting for social changes which might remove them.[15]

Summers wrongly exempts Heagney and her centres from this critique. She admits that the education courses they offered left something to be desired; housewifery, drawing, singing and elocution sound more like training for Jane Austen heroines than job training during the Depression. Had the UGRM survived, Summers argues, it might have been able to grapple with the dilemma. But the dilemma lay in the welfare approach itself.

As with refuges and rape crisis centres in more recent times, the 1930s welfare approach saw women essentially as victims needing help. Rather than mobilising a large political fighting force, they concentrated on helping the needy or retraining the few. They offered the unemployed bandaids for their wounds, when they needed weapons and organisation for a fightback.

Some might argue that there was no basis for such a fightback – that, since they lacked union organisation and were weighed down by their household cares, it would be utopian to expect women of the time to have done more than

South Maitland Unemployed Women's Bureau May Day 1930s

OMENS BUREAU
DISTRICT
STARVATION
FOR THE MANY
OF THE LYONS &
GER GOVERNMENTS

whimper quietly and submit. Summers gives us a picture of Heagney taking a principled feminist stand in splendid isolation: 'But there was little she could do for she had virtually no support.' Power, similarly, refers to the small group of Sydney feminists as 'voices in the wilderness.'[16]

I take a contrary position. If we restrict ourselves to looking for clear articulation of feminist principles, we will find very few examples. But if we look for the participation of women in the struggles of the day, then we will find that they did not remain hidden or in the background.

Unemployed women organise

Many modern accounts of the unemployed movement focus on the helpless wife, baby in arms, sitting on her pathetic possessions in the street after being evicted. At best, they show women as fundraisers. Actually, women played a very active role in the unemployed movement.

Edna Ryan, for example, describes speaking at numerous street meetings in Sydney:

> We always got a good reception and had good meetings. It was relatively easy then to organise the unemployed because they queued up to get their dole and met each other regularly and were able to talk about current affairs and make plans for whatever meetings were on.[17]

Although sustenance and relief was for men only, government support was distributed at local government level, so local pressure could be brought to bear. In Boolaroo NSW, in September 1930, a women's demonstration marched on the local police station demanding relief for unemployed women. Port Adelaide had a women's unemployed committee, with 150 attending meetings. After one meeting, over 100 pursued a scab. In another incident, a female picket was described as 'jumping on the back' of a scab and 'bearing him to the ground, scratching and screaming.' When a teacher at a Port Adelaide school kept some children in to write 500 words each for using the word 'scab' during a wharf strike, several hundred women marched on the school in protest and had to be stopped by police.[18]

This militancy continued throughout the Depression. At a demonstration by the Newcastle Unemployed Workers' Movement (UWM) in 1932, the jobless were 'so incensed' that they forced the doors of the local bureau and demanded an interview:

A big part was played by the women who, during the abuse from officials, were advised to leave by the police 'in case of trouble' but refused stating, 'If there is to be trouble, we will take our share of it!'

The demonstrators won their demands, including immediate relief for six women and a man with a sick wife and an 8-day-old child. In the same year, when police tried to assault male unemployed leaders at a meeting in Glebe (Sydney):

> the women took a prominent part in the defence, one was knocked over and tramped over by policemen, but this did not deter her from still carrying on her protest against police brutality.[19]

During the 1935 relief workers' strike, there were several similar accounts. At Como (NSW), the wives not only organised social functions and collected money and food, but also wrote articles and marched in demonstrations. On one occasion, police stopped a march of unemployed men in Corrimal:

> When this became known to the women they immediately took the lead and marched over three miles to the [North Illawarra] council chambers, which they packed to the limit. The mayor was asked to receive a deputation of women and a speaker which he refused. It was then the trouble started. The whole audience crowded behind the chairs of the aldermen demanding the women be heard.
>
> The mayor threatened to have the room cleared if they were not quiet, but the women told him he could have them locked up, at least they would be fed, and they would take their children along too, and they could feed them also; that even if their menfolk were on strike they didn't intend to starve. A further demonstration was arranged by the men and the women to the Food Relief Depot at Wollongong, which resulted in a complete victory for the strikers, for besides receiving food relief for the time they were on strike, the men were also reinstated.[20]

It appears that women were not as active in the Melbourne dole strike as they were in NSW. However: 'in many instances they have been leading and marching in the demonstrations. They took part in an illegal demonstration from North Melbourne Town Hall.' One article claimed that they 'were clamouring for a share in the work. One hundred of them marched to a charity organisation and demanded relief.' However, they did not participate fully in the local committees. A few women were active in almost every suburb, but they did little more than collect relief: 'only in one or two places did they address meetings or go on the picket line'. The reason for this seems to have been that, in some suburbs (such as Port Melbourne), the strike leaders actually refused to allow them onto the committees. However, the author remarked that, where the strikers were most solid (such as in Richmond), the greatest numbers of women were drawn into strike activity.[21]

Another popular tactic was deputations to members of parliament:

The politicians hated to see the women...oh they hated them...biggest cowards on earth, all the blah, blah, blah in the world but they couldn't stand up to the women. When you're hungry and you can't feed your children you get pretty angry.[22]

Women were also active in the eviction struggles. In Melbourne's inner suburbs, the UWM was very well organised and, according to its well-known leader Jim Munro, stopped many evictions. The police caught them in Fitzroy once and 'belted the insides out of us; men, women and children'. On another occasion, when some furniture had been seized to pay overdue rent, UWM members went around to make sure that no regular secondhand dealer would bid for it at the auction. This was successful, but they were worried about some 'ladies' who had also turned up at the auction:

Our wives and everybody got alongside them and growled, 'You bid for this you bitch, and I'll tear your bloody hair out'. 'You open your mouth and I'll kick your guts in!'

The furniture was safely returned to the dispossessed family.[23]

While men appear to have been the main organising force behind anti-eviction actions, the women didn't always wait for them to act. When a Footscray family was to be evicted in 1935, the husband went as an individual to the local authorities – only to be told to be out before Christmas. But the women of the district:

had made up their minds that no eviction was going to take place, and they elected a deputation to wait on the Town Clerk and place the case in its stark reality before him.

This tactic was successful – and just in time, because the wife gave birth that day.[24]

Events in 1930 highlight the courage of these female activists. Acting under orders from the NSW Lang Labor government, police arrested a number of women. Pat Hurd, the daughter of communist writer Jean Devanny, was only 17:

> So we called this fantastic meeting in the Lower Town Hall. And that was my debut as a speaker, in front of all these hundreds of unemployed women.
>
> We decided we'd have a march up to parliament house and present a deputation... This huge big police inspector with all his policemen standing across the roadway called upon us to stop and read us the riot act...and then asked us to desist and go home. None of us would do it. Some women lay down on tram lines. One woman started fighting a policeman with an umbrella and there was great melee, oh a terrific fight. All these hundreds of women – the traffic was held up right back to the railway station.

Although she had been standing on the sidelines, Pat was arrested:

> Then they started to drag me...through the streets of Sydney. And I got indignant... So I started to punch one of the blokes and hit him with the handcuffs. He said, 'That's assaulting the police. That's another charge.'

Support For Men.

The secretary of the Wonthaggi Miners' Federation (Mr. I. Williams) headed the band of workers and their wives who marched to the Sunbeam pithead this afternoon. As a demonstration, they pledged support to the strikers and demanded Government action to compel payment of award rates.

A state of strike began to-day on the surface in three of the five pits on the Jumbunna-Korumburra field. About 150 men are involved.

In jail, they decided to show their solidarity with a number of male eviction fighters, who had been framed and sentenced to 6–9 months, by joining them in a hunger strike:

> It was an act of solidarity with these wrongly arrested anti-eviction fighters. Some of the women were so weak they had to be taken to hospital and forcibly fed at four days. I lasted the longest... I finished my eight days' hunger strike. [25]

Such activity had a lasting impact. One reminisced:

> We were always fighting and demonstrating in those days. It made me a militant...you had to get into the struggle to survive...we were all in it together...although we had nothing...you didn't have time to think of your own troubles. [26]

This militancy was not simply instigated by men. In fact, women often resisted their husbands' attempts to protect them from violence:

> The men were having street meetings too. It was illegal you see...there was no free speech. My husband told me not to come up to town this night as there was going to be trouble. Well, I dressed my son up when he went off, and off I went. I was walking up the street when this big policeman ordered me off. Someone yelled that Paddy was in gaol...well, I was furious, I turned on the policeman and stamped my feet at him and told him, how dare you speak to me like that amongst other things. Everyone was clapping and singing out...anyway, he backed off and never arrested me. [27]

Brazen hussies and strike support

There are many cases of female support for male strikers. In the seamen's strike of 1936, a Seamen's Wives' Strike Committee of 20 in Melbourne seems to have collected and distributed strike relief as its main activity. The committee secretary said:

> It makes you laugh to hear that men ought to go back to work for the sake of their womenfolk. This is our strike as much as it is the men's. [28]

In her novel *Sugar Heaven*, Jean Devanny describes the wives' role in the Queensland sugar cane cutters' strike of 1935.[29]

Best known and most inspiring, however, is the Miners' Women's Auxiliary. Miners' wives have a tradition of action from the 19th century: they stopped trains carrying scabs, marched and picketed, argued with scabs and 'tin-kettled' (banging on pots and pans in a war of nerves). Such was their reputation that they were rebuked for 'forgetting their sex'. In one strike, the manager allowed the men strikers to address the scabs but refused the women.[30]

During the Depression, this tradition developed into formal organisation. The 1934 Wonthaggi strike saw the first women's auxiliary. In the following years, auxiliaries sprang up in many mining centres. However, the national leadership did not recognise them until 1939. This suggests some reluctance by the officials to endorse an organisation which might 'interfere with the domestic work of the union'. There was hesitation at the rank and file level as well:

> Lots of the men didn't like their women taking up public action... We used to go to Lodge [Union branch] meetings and address them. Some of the men were embarrassed and so were we but we soon got used to each other.[31]

Sometimes, the men put up more of a fight:

> I remember I heard about a meeting being held that night and decided to go. We had built a shack and it only had one door. My husband sat in the doorway so I couldn't go, but I was only about 6 stone so I slipped out the window and away down the road I went...he was alright after that...got used to it and always minded the children so I could be in all the meetings and demonstrations.[32]

Activities included picketing, demonstrating, petitions, raising money, press conferences and speaking on the radio. Even the soup kitchens and socials took on a political character during the long strikes of 1939 and 1949 in NSW. Despite the term 'auxiliary', this was obviously a case of the women organising in their own right and in their own interests:

> It wasn't that the Women's Auxiliary just supported men...it was our own survival we were fighting for... I tell you it built character, those struggles... Somehow when you're in your own little family everything

REBEL WOMEN

Women textile workers strike Launceston August 1932. Clockwise from top: picketing at Patons & Baldwins mill; E. Clarke, member of the strike committee; young women strikers 'on the grass'; crowd listening to TWU Branch Secretary Cyril Smith at rear of Trades Hall.

BRAZEN HUSSIES AND GOD'S POLICE

just goes along and you nestle in. When everything is an upheaval...it's different...everyone is together.

They called us brazen hussies...it was unheard of...the coalfields women didn't take long to cotton on...basically they were fighters ...they had to be.[33]

The brazen hussies probably found the president of the Miners' Federation pretty paternalistic, when the auxiliary was finally recognised nationally in 1939:

In the past, women folk have been isolated from an industrial point of view and to some extent have indirectly assisted the ruling class on account of their lack of knowledge and understanding of the class struggle. Lately however considerable progress has been made by their support of the Federation in the national strike.[34]

Never let the facts spoil a good prejudice!

Other unions set up women's auxiliaries during the thirties. But they were more orientated to conventional activities and do not seem to have had the spontaneous and fiery militant quality of those in the mining communities. Members of the Australian Railways Union auxiliary baked their own bread against price rises (and won a reduction of one penny). They also had a clothes fund for babies of mothers on the dole. They did participate in a big rally in the Sydney Domain, protesting about the dismissal of married women. In some country centres, the women's auxiliary was the main focus for the union.[35]

Striking back

There seems to have been almost a continuous battle between textile employers and workers throughout the Depression. It started in August 1932, when Victorian employers cut wages by 15 percent – in addition to the 10 percent across-the-board cut for all workers two years previously.

Immediately, 700 employees at Yarra Falls Spinning Mills, 500 of them female, went on strike. Following an offer to reduce the cut to 7.5 percent, the union officials convinced the strikers to return to work, pending further negotiations. Not long afterwards, at a mass meeting which consisted 'largely of young women and girls and boys dressed in knickerbockers', 1,000 textile workers voted to strike again, electing a committee which sent speakers out to other mills to spread the strike. On the same day, the dispute spread to Launceston, where

1,000 workers from three mills struck. When the rain set in, picketers pitched tents in the street.

With 3,500 out in Melbourne, there were too many to meet in Trades Hall, so 'the strikers went to the Temperance Hall, the girls marching along Russell Street singing.' The strike was solid and the mood determined; unfortunately, inexperience and lack of organisation in Melbourne allowed the union officials to independently talk members in Ballarat and Geelong into accepting the offer. Officials carried out none of the rank and file decisions about leaflets and picketing. The strike ended in Melbourne after 10 days and in Tasmania six days later. Although forced to settle, workers had achieved a partial victory in reducing the cut to 7.5 percent.[36]

A little over a year later, a second important mass strike occurred in the same industry – this time in NSW. The issue was a new award which meant wage cuts, a speedup and night work for women. The strike started in Orange, where there were 'disorderly scenes':

> A party of more than twenty girls...went in search of other girls who had offered for work that morning. They shouted insulting names at the loyal workers. Then they went in a body to a hotel, where another worker boarded, and sought to gain entrance to her room. Sergeant Roser seized the leader of the girls and conducted her to the police station in a car.[37]

With the spread to Goulburn and Sydney came much active picketing and fundraising. Again, the union officials 'on many occasions...completely ignored the strike committee and...prevented it exercising direction and control of the strike'. Again, the strike ended with only a partial victory, despite a militant mood that could have taken it to complete success. The full operation of the new award was prevented in most mills, but there were some losses. A number of smaller stopworks and disputes occurred in the wake of the major strike; for example, workers at the Commonwealth Weaving Mills in Sydney were able to prevent victimisations, but they could not be averted at a number of other mills.[38]

A third wave of strikes occurred in early 1938, again in Victoria. There was a range of issues, including dismissals and night shift rates, but the strikes focused on piece rates in the new award. About 2,500 workers were involved altogether, many of them women and juniors, and, as each mill settled, another would go out. Although some workplaces elected strike committees, control passed to the Trades Hall after the first few days. The workers seem to have won substantial wage increases.[39]

Group of Melbourne textile workers 1932

In fact, the textile industry was seldom free of disputes during the 1930s, and the daily press regularly reported smaller strikes. Part of the explanation for the militancy in this industry might be the fact that unemployment peaked earlier in the sector than in manufacturing industry generally. Having gone into recession in 1927, the textile industry was recovering strongly by 1931–32 because of devaluation and tariffs. Employers could, therefore, afford minor concessions not available in other sectors. Minority Movement members were active in the first and second strike wave, and their agitation seems to have had some effect.

The clothing industry also had a large female workforce. Organising in this industry was much more difficult than in textiles, because workshops were smaller and sweatshop conditions common. Further, piecework and outwork must have undermined efforts to organise into unions. The union officials' role in suppressing incipient militancy was also an obstacle. Although the Militant Minority Movement distributed leaflets to clothing workers during the 1932 strike, they never found a foothold in the industry.

All the same, there were instances of industrial action. A one-week strike in a Melbourne factory in 1930 gained a new weekly wage based on the previous piece rates. Workers in at least one other factory were also able to prevent a wage cut.[40]

A larger dispute occurred in July 1932, when clothing workers were again faced with a wage cutting award in addition to the 10 percent across-the-board cut. The union's strength was concentrated in men's ready-made clothing, and about 700 of these workers, mostly women, engaged in a short-lived strike. They reluctantly returned to work under pressure from the union officials, who convinced a mass meeting to accept the employers' offer of a restoration of wages. This led to defeat, because the employers never carried out their promise.[41]

A new system involving speedup led to a strike in March 1935 by 170 young women from three men's clothing factories. After 10 days out, they went back, to the comment from the union secretary, one Mr A. Wallis, that: 'the new system… would benefit both employers and employees'. A short strike at Universal Clothing in July 1937 did win a retrospective wage rise.[42]

Female rubber workers engaged in a number of strikes. An Act banning mass picketing allowed police to disband daily pickets at Hardie Rubber Works in June 1930. Several years later, 180 women at the same factory struck over piece work rates. When the strikers went to collect their previous week's wages, the police surrounded them in an attempt, as a union official put it, to create a 'fear psychology'.[43] When another group of 500 strikers rejected a union executive recommendation to return to work, the case went to arbitration. The judge commented:

It is deplorable that a big and important union like this one, which has always given assistance to this court in all industrial matters should be defied by a handful of women who are nothing but rebels.[44]

The executive responded that it was doing everything in its power to persuade them to return to work.

Following the dismissal of two female tobacco workers in May 1935, approximately 50 strikers held out for over a year. A levy on others in the industry provided strike pay, and the matter came up in parliament after police used violence to break up a picket. The union clearly gave a fair degree of support, including sending delegates interstate to publicise their case and forming a 'flying squad' to visit tobacconists. Since the factory resumed production with scabs

WOMEN'S RALLY.

Tumult and Uproar.

WILD SCENES AT ADYAR HALL.

The women's meeting convened by the Industrial Peace Association at Adyar Hall last night began and ended in tumult. It was one of the most uproarious meetings of women that has taken place in Sydney, and perhaps eclipsed any as a demonstration of personal and class hostility.

No one speaker was heard for more than a few consecutive seconds before she was either counted out, howled down, or her voice drowned in the chorus of "Solidarity for Ever."

Long before the meeting started the hall was booming with the sound of loud-voiced within three weeks of the strike's commencement, the only hope of victory lay in spreading the strike. Although they seem to have considered this action, it never actually occurred.[45]

A number of other industries also saw women take industrial action. In 1935, there was a strike at Melbourne basket shoe factories over the demand to be covered by the bootmakers' award. Most of the strikers were European migrants. Pantry maids at Carlyons Restaurant in Melbourne's Spencer Street campaigned successfully against overtime and victimisation, with most joining the union. In Sydney, there was also a successful campaign to organise hotel and restaurant workers. Railway waitresses met in October 1937 to discuss several grievances and formed a section of the Australian Railways Union. In 1933, Western Australian domestic servants gained the right to be addressed as Miss or Mrs.[46]

Given that there was industrial action in most occupations where women were found, it is clear that it is quite mistaken to say:

> Lack of trade union and other organised support meant that women fared badly, for the more strongly organised sections of the community were pacified at the expense of those less able to defend their rights.[47]

Certainly, their unions were often weak; nonetheless, there was a substantial level of rank and file action. In many cases, women strikers received adequate and even quite good support from their union officials. If they or their unions lacked the power and political awareness to create a really effective overall response to the economic and social crisis of the 1930s, then so, after all, did most men.

Right-wing women organise

Radical and working-class women weren't the only ones to organise. In opposition to, and frequently in conflict with, them was the Australian Women's Guild of Empire, launched in 1929 under the capable and experienced leadership of Adela Pankhurst Walsh.

Daughter of the famous British suffragette, Emmeline Pankhurst, Adela came out to Australia in 1915. Originally a militant socialist and feminist, and briefly a member of the young Communist Party, she had swung sharply to the right by the end of the 1920s. Not only was she now for industrial peace; she had also left behind any support for women's rights, claiming that these women were sapping the initiative of men who had 'spilled their blood over the whole surface of the earth, and strewn their bones thick beneath every sea in the interests of future generations.'[48]

The Guild hoped to 'end the industrial and class strife and to restore industry on a basis of cooperation and good will.' Although the first point of its charter was 'to combat communism and all forms of class government', one is not really surprised to find Lady Rhondda and Lady Gordon as its patronesses. Mrs David Maugham, daughter of Australia's first (conservative) prime minister and married to a prominent lawyer, was president for several years, and names prominent in Sydney's social and business world were conspicuous among the membership. Turnover in the executive resulted not from ideological differences but from the resignations of ladies leaving for overseas trips. The NSW Chamber of Manufacturers gave it consistent financial support, and other employers' organisations contributed in various ways.[49]

In its early years, the Guild was very active among working-class housewives in the industrial suburbs of Sydney and nearby centres such as Wollongong. At 'industrial tea parties' (where free food and entertainment were drawcards), the wives of unemployed men obtained fabric at cheap rates, to be made into clothes and then sold by the Guild. There were also weekly meetings, children's circles ('little outposts of empire') and charity work.

The Guild was anathema to the Communist Party, who constantly reviled Adela Walsh. The CPA's Militant Women's Group called her 'Mrs Liar Walsh' or 'Mrs Traitor Walsh' in their publications, and the Sydney and Cessnock groups followed her around to her various meetings to expose her politics. The Guild answered the insults in kind, attacking 'Madam Kollontai and her shrieking sisterhood.'[50]

One tea party in Millers Point (Sydney) in 1934 proved 'a most unpleasant afternoon.' The secretary reported:

> The Communist Women, led by Mrs Jean Devanny came in a body and interrupted continuously... We all felt proud to belong to the Guild when we listened to Mrs Walsh quietly answering the avalanche of questions that was hurled at her while honestly trying to help these people.[51]

Most of the Guild's efforts went into the workplace. At the invitation of employers, Adela and others would speak to lunch hour meetings in shops, at factories and on the docks. A speaker at the Alexandria Spinning Mills in 1937 focused on the urgent need for Australia to remain loyal to the empire. At the end of the meeting, she sold her audience wool to make winter bed covers for those unable to afford them.[52]

These factory incursions often provoked hostility. At one meeting at IXL in 1936, the Guild speaker managed to overcome the resentment:

'What do you want here?' hooted an interjector. 'You never wash a cup!' 'You couldn't do a day's washing!' screamed others. Hastily Mrs Metcalfe held up her flag of battle – a large double bed quilt made from knitted squares... [She] explained that this quilt was made by cooperation and loving friendship. Only by cooperation could success be achieved. First of all in the home, and then in industry, by cooperation between capital, management and labour.[53]

On earlier occasions in the same factory, the Guild came off second best. Adela as the speaker was heckled:

'If you want work, come and work like us.'

'Twister! How much are you paid for this?'

Adela started to speak: 'I only wish to get more work for the unemployed...' But the indignant workers howled her down and made her get out. We looked over the wall and saw Adela and her friend running down the lane.

This may not have been the entirely spontaneous action it was claimed to be. But, as one participant said: 'There is not one communist in this factory, but there is not one of us would stand a twister like her.'[54]

Whenever there was a strike, Adela would appear, speak to the workers and hand out leaflets. Not surprisingly, she was popular with employers, who got into the habit of sending for her at the first whiff of industrial action. By 1936, she was addressing 30 audiences a month as well as speaking every Sunday in the Domain.[55]

The Guild was not the only right-wing women's organisation of the period. In September 1931, an anti-communist meeting in the Sydney Town Hall included the women's section of the Sane Democracy League, the Feminist League, the National Association of Women, the Women' Christian Temperance Union and the Progressive Housewives' Association. They all wished to take the offensive to defend Country, Religion and Morality; marriage itself would be smashed if left-wing 'fiends' had their way. The meeting carried a motion demanding the 'expulsion of communism from this country, vigorously, unconditionally and uncompromisingly'. The disruption of the meeting by radical women, presumably members of the CPA, led to 'wild scenes':

> Seven women were ejected. One fought a constable with her fists, and others attacked the police with their handbags. They shouted at the top of their voices while they were being ejected.[56]

So much for the picture of 'mute' women in the Depression! In reality, they played many roles, including that of working-class fighters. They were to do so again in the World War that followed.

Above: Recruitment poster for women's auxiliary services and essential war work. Typical of such posters, the women have been airbrushed and appear pretty, well-groomed, feminine and cheerful. Left: Front cover Australian Women's Weekly 9 October 1943 attempts to show you can look glamorous while working on machinery.

Class struggle on the home front
Women, unions and militancy in the Second World War

JANEY STONE

Winnie the War-Winner was Australia's answer to Rosie the Riveter. Feminine yet patriotic, she entered paid employment not for her own sake, but to support the war effort and her soldier husband:

> Hats off to these women! No one who has not seen them can possibly appreciate how great is their contribution to the nation's war effort... In one factory I saw a girl who had come straight from a beauty parlour. She was doing work that was dirty and hard on the hands. When she was asked how she found the work after a beauty parlour, she said she liked it much better... 'It's much more interesting and besides – I'm making cartridges for my husband to fire'.[1]

The content of propaganda varied at different stages of the war. From the outbreak of war in September 1939 until Pearl Harbour in December 1941, there was no absolute shortage of labour. The transfer of labour from one sector to another sufficed, and the propaganda emphasis was mainly on thrift and self-sacrifice. While the use of makeup had to be curtailed ('The girl...who hoards cosmetics... is plainly speaking a traitor to her country, to other women and to her true self'), looking stiff or masculine 'is what every feminine girl will always try to avoid', since 'women who are careless about their looks are often careless about their jobs'. At this stage, the authorities resisted pressure to create service branches for women, trying to divert patriotic urges into knitting socks and rolling bandages.[2]

After Pearl Harbour, there *was* an absolute shortage of labour. The armed forces and defence production expanded, and Australia was expected to feed US forces in the Pacific. Cabinet endorsed 'the extensive employment of women.'

Promotion for "victory jobs" in the Women's Weekly April 1943

They set up the Women's Employment Board (WEB), registered women for employment and launched a major recruitment campaign. The *Women's Weekly* announced: 'Australia is calling on her women as never before',[3] and posters urged them to 'take a Victory job':

> You'll find it no harder than your house job. Easier perhaps. In fact, many war production factories, with their spic-and-span canteens, bright music and carefully-planned rest breaks are more fun to work in than any house.[4]

The *Women's Weekly* reoriented to an industrial audience. The appointment of the magazine's top management, Frank Packer and Edward Theodore, to the Allied Works Council (created to solve 'manpower problems') around that time may not have been a coincidence. The *Weekly* now emphasised factory work and femininity at the same time:

When doing our job on munitions we don't neglect our appearance – but still keep our feminine charm by always having our Escapade lipstick with us.[5]

Such charm was a moral obligation, because 'Grooming...not only promotes but sustains morale.'[6]

By late 1943, the threat of invasion was largely removed. Except in the rural sector, the demand for labour eased. Postwar expectations were to the fore, and articles asking: 'What will women do when the war is over?' were common. Employers kept reminding employees that their jobs were only for the duration. The manager at the Maribyrnong Ordnance Factory wrote:

> The questions are often asked... Are the women of any real value in industry or are they merely a temporary expedient brought into being during the war period? The answer to both is yes.[7]

By 1945, the *Women's Weekly* was announcing a 'new era of feminine loveliness'.[8]

Winnie the War-Winner was thrifty at home, hard working and uncomplaining. She was called upon to be men's equal, but only temporarily. She had to do long hours of dirty work, yet remain feminine. Everyone would recognise her essential contribution, but she would receive less pay than men. The new job gave confidence, but the only outlet offered was more knitting and new ways to cook rabbit. She must, at all times, remember the boys in the trenches, yet she must never behave like them.[9]

Winnie was only a myth. Let's look at the reality.

From the florist to the factory floor

The war period was one of restructuring and rationalisation. New technology, increased need for precision and greater specialisation meant big changes in factories. Conveyor belt flow systems became much more common, and there was a marked increase in the number of semi-skilled metal workers. Employers regarded female labour as very suited to the changed conditions.[10] The propaganda reflected the dilemma the changes generated. Government and employers wanted female labour but maintained an eye on postwar conditions.

After the bombing of Pearl Harbour, a proposal to cabinet suggested:

> necessary supplies of female labour can be obtained without offering men's wages, particularly if appeal is made to patriotic sentiment... It is probable also that a substantial supply of female labour could be secured for munitions and other industries without departing from the present principles regarding the payment of females.[11]

An employers' representative on the Manpower Committee believed that it would be easy to 'send the women home at the end of the war'.[12] But the constant reiteration of the images only shows the propagandists' underlying lack of confidence. Nor was this attempted manipulation due only to the sexism of the bosses or authorities (still mostly male). Wartime capitalist society manipulated both genders in the 'national interest', although more overtly than in peacetime. The prevailing ideology was still essentially the interest of capital.

The frequently raised concept of the 'reserve army of labour' – the idea that women were sent from the home into the workforce during the war only to be returned to domesticity at its end – places too much reliance on this propaganda. Propaganda is not the same as reality. The audience were not mindless automatons. Although social pressure was high, those who went to work did so for their own reasons and were not the simple victims of manipulation. One study shows that, during the war, age, marital status and class were the main determinants of whether women entered the workforce.[13]

The 'reserve army of labour' theory is also a numerical oversimplification. The female proportion of the workforce had risen steadily for decades. As early as 1927, about half of all factory workers in Australia were female; in Victoria, they made up 65 percent. Early in the century, they worked mostly in the traditional areas, such as clothing, textiles, shoes and food preserving. In the 1920s–30s, they began to move into metal and engineering, where they did 'light repetitive work' such as core-making, drilling and assembling.[14]

However, change was much more rapid during the war. Between July 1939 and June 1945, the female 'working population' (those employed, actively seeking work or in the armed services) increased from 677,500 to 811,200. Natural increase can account for some of this. The number of females 'not normally seeking occupation who have become breadwinners' peaked at around 99,300 in June 1943. This is the best estimate of the number who went from being housewives to entering paid employment. More important than the move from the home was the change in the *type* of work. Most moved from self-employment, domestic work (as servants) and unemployment to being wage and salary earners. This category increased from 64.5 percent to 80.1 percent of the female working population between 1939 and 1943, while domestic servants declined from 18.3 percent in 1939 to 5.9 percent in 1945. A 1941 survey of 780 women in a South Australian munitions factory illustrates this change: 34 percent had been domestic servants, 24 percent factory workers, and others shop assistants, waitresses, nurses, domestics and clerks. Only 47 (6 percent) had not previously been employed. The other important change was that many were now married; married females' participation rate more than doubled between 1933 and 1945.[15]

During that period, all industrial sectors of the economy experienced a decrease in masculinity (proportion of the workforce male), but it was most marked in government munitions factories and in banking and insurance. In the metal industry, where a massive increase in demand for war equipment and munitions combined with large numbers of men leaving industry to go into the armed forces, the number of women rose from 1,375 in 1933 to 52,847 in 1943. By 1945, they made up 13 percent of all workers in the industry.[16]

1st September, 1943.

The Editor,
"Sydney Morning Herald".

Dear Sir,

We hear of constant shortages of women workers for various types of vital work, and apparently we have arrived at no satisfactory way to obtain these workers. There is one obvious way to attract workers to any occupation - namely, to raise the pay earned in that occupation.

Facts and figures show that nursing, domestic work, restaurant work, and work in textile and other low-paid factory employment, are definitely occupations which are not attractive to women. The way to make them so is to offer wages and conditions in line with other work which is performed, and which is often of less value to the community.

Women workers have been under-paid and exploited in the past. They have shown their capacity and efficiency for the Services, in defence works, and in replacing men workers in various occupations. The time has arrived when women's work must be valued at the same ratio as men's work. For instance, it is absurd that the pay of a nurse, with all her skill and responsibility, should be less than the man's basic wage.

Make the payment fit the qualifications and nature of the work, and there will be no shortage of women workers.

Yours faithfully,

(Jessie M. G. Street)

Letter from Jessie Street to the *Sydney Morning Herald* arguing for equal pay

More women were working, doing what had previously been men's work, and receiving better wages. The same 1941 factory survey found that the 'girls were obviously attracted by high wages offering in munitions work and the vast majority were prepared to do overtime for extra pay'. The average weekly wage in munitions was £3.3.0 ($6.30), compared to the average previous wage of those surveyed of £1.7.6½ ($2.75).[17]

This raises the most vexed issue in the new industrial climate. When the government set up the WEB in 1942, its charter was to encourage and regulate the employment of women in work usually done by men or in new war jobs. It had to set hours and determine any special conditions.[18] But the impact of the WEB was mainly felt when it had to set wages in the non-traditional and new jobs. This it did, based on:

> the efficiency of females in the performance of the work and any other special factors which may be likely to affect the productivity of their work in relation to that of males.[19]

The words 'efficiency' and 'productivity' opened the door to piecework in some areas. But the actual pay rates themselves were most important.

The minimum rate for adult females had been fixed at 54 percent of the male basic wage by the historic Harvester award in 1907. The WEB regulations now required it to set wages at between 60 percent and 100 percent. While a few workers, such as tram conductresses, clerical workers and some in retail won 100 percent, most awards were for 90 percent. The employers did everything they could to get the WEB to decide on less. Led by the Metal Trades Employers' Association, they fought hard against the Board and many of its decisions. There were numerous attacks in the High Court. Twice, the Board had to suspend sittings when the Senate disallowed regulations. The employers used delaying tactics at hearings and frequently refused to implement decisions for higher wages. They claimed that women needed more supervision and were less productive because of their lesser strength and greater absenteeism. One tactic was to slightly redefine jobs so that women weren't quite doing the full work of men. Another was to break the job down so that it entailed less responsibility.[20]

This pressure seems to have influenced the WEB itself. The Board commented on one application:

> The evidence is that the woman has done practically the whole of the work of an oiler and greaser and has been prevented from doing the full

amount of work by reason of some restrictions that the employers think fit to impose upon her, possibly out of regard for a feeling that she might not be capable of climbing a high ladder. She says she is able to do it and we have no doubt she is capable of doing it. We think she should not be prevented from earning the full award rate.[21]

She still only got 90 percent.

Lynn Beaton notes that there was no serious opposition to the conscription of women into low-paid jobs; yet, there was bitter resistance both to WEB rates and to the WEB's very existence. The opposition was not so much to women working, but to their entering new fields and receiving higher wages.[22]

The wartime environment challenged all classes and institutions. The rest of this chapter concentrates on the response of the working class and its institutions to women's new role and briefly considers the response of upper-class women.

Dilution and unionisation

Important though they are in defending workers' rights, unions are part of the capitalist system, devoted to improving conditions within the system but not to overturning it. Accordingly, full-time officials find themselves in a contradictory position. On the one hand, their livelihood depends on their making gains for workers. On the other hand, their interests are tied up with the institution (their union), so they form a conservative layer which accepts the existing social order and tends to restrain militant struggles which might challenge it.[23]

The ideological pressure on the working class during the war was tremendous. All society's institutions lined up behind the war effort. The leadership of most unions joined in the mainstream propaganda, supporting the 'battle for production'. The Federated Ironworkers (FIA), for example, campaigned hard against strikes. When strikes did break out, support from the union structure was almost non-existent. The leadership called for 'increased discipline' to deal with the 'larrikin element' on the waterfront:

> We should not wait for the boss to sack these people, but we should sack them ourselves if they are not prepared to mend their ways and pull their full weight.[24]

Women workers at the Commonwealth Aircraft Factory, Fisherman's Bend (Melbourne)

Officials were not always so rigid. The Tramways Association in Melbourne had a lengthy dispute over staffing and long hours, including a stopwork meeting on football Grand Final Day in 1944. The Vice-president justified wartime industrial action, declaring:

> If tramways employees are not prepared to make the small sacrifice of a stopwork meeting, the future of the men who are fighting will be jeopardised.[25]

By and large, however, workers fighting to defend their rights during the war faced great resistance from their full-time officials and from fellow workers heavily influenced by this propaganda.

The entry of women into a previously male domain was a complicating factor. Although craft unions in the non-traditional areas had long resisted this, and the wartime influx generated more outright sexism,[26] the reactions of male unionists cannot be ascribed simply to sensitive male egos. Mostly, their response to female labour was also tied up with traditional union principles. These were often the narrow principles of craft unionism. Sometimes, the unions' attitude was conditioned by their limited aims in a social crisis they didn't understand – as in the Depression.

Despite the wartime exigencies, the Amalgamated Engineering Union (AEU) never gave up the right to strike, although the leading body was 'perturbed' when workers struck before informing officials.[27] The Australian AEU was a branch of the British union until 1968. It was an old organisation with long traditions. Engineers were craft conscious – proud of their skills and standards of work. The AEU was comparatively wealthy and, before World War II, provided many non industrial benefits such as insurance against loss of tools, accidents,

sickness and unemployment. Although the number of unskilled worker members was growing slowly, historian Tom Sheridan says: 'there is no doubt that the AEU remained predominantly a craft union right to the end of its separate existence in 1972.' Its attitude to women in the industry and as members was conditioned by its basic outlook. Sheridan explains:

> As with all other unions, the AEU's *raison d'être* was to guard and improve its members' conditions of work. Within the policy structure erected on that premise the major influence was the fear of unemployment... Their long experience of the cruel trade cycle naturally made them hesitate for a considerable period before finally accepting that the 1940s had ushered in a new era of full employment. Most engineers' doubts disappeared only in the late 1950s and their long conditioning has continued to call forth most of the old automatic reflexes into the seventies.[28]

One of the 'old automatic reflexes' was opposition to women. Sheridan shows how this opposition was tied up with fears bred by experience, particularly of job losses.

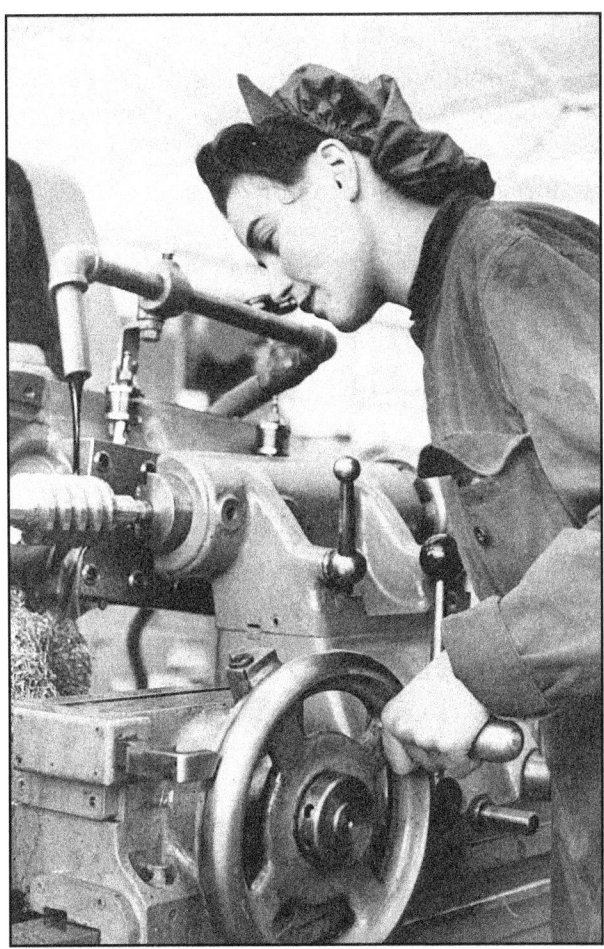

Women munition factory workers (left) are various ages and focussed on their work. But Mildred Thornten (right), lathe operator, with her glamorous hair and her makeup, looks posed.

During World War I, Britain had experienced a rapid influx of (male) engineers who hadn't had the long training previously considered necessary to do tradesmen's work. In World War II, the AEU was determined to have more control over these 'dilutees'. It negotiated with the government very early on and reached an agreement in 1940 allowing (male) 'dilution'. Policy in the early 1940s was:

> designed for the immediate and future safeguarding of its own membership, whose economic interests constitute the primary concern of the organisation. Second preference in employment was to be given to men disemployed through war conditions; and, thirdly, the employment of women was approved, provided that they be paid the male rate for the job. If and when normal conditions return it was assumed that the

reverse order would prevail in discharges from the industry in line with the time-honoured practice of last on first off, taking it for granted that this represented a natural order of priority in industrial status.[29]

Increasing numbers of females in the industry in the early 1940s created a dilemma. The rules precluded their admission, but both officials and rank and filers knew that the presence of unorganised workers weakens a union's position. The AEU couldn't negotiate for them; but, in order to protect its members' own wages, it had to ensure equal pay. From 1940, despite continuing sexism on the shop floor, there was mounting pressure up through the union structure to change the rules.[30]

Resisting 'dilution' meant that AEU members had to fill the extra demand for labour as much as possible themselves, by working long hours and making efforts to 'supplement the 44-hour week with as much overtime as the human form can stand'. Their position on 'dilution' meant that the union was unable to protect members' interests in this situation. Not only couldn't it look after their health; it couldn't even use overtime bans as a tactical weapon. In early 1941, the AEU refused to be associated with an overtime ban as part of a campaign against new tax provisions. In the end, the government was forced to intervene and limit hours to 56 per week.[31]

This situation, together with the increasing numbers of unorganised workers on the shop floor, led to pressure to admit women. In Britain, AEU shop stewards helped to organise women into other unions.[32] In Australia, by 1940, organisers (who were close to the shop floor) were putting pressure on the leadership. The initial reply was a flat no 'on principle'. However, by April 1941, they were pressuring the executive committee in Britain for permission to organise females 'for our own protection'. London refused, but district officials kept up the pressure in Australia. Eventually, there was an international ballot in July 1942, although bureaucratic hold-ups delayed the rule change until April 1943.

At that point, the AEU moved quickly to 'unionise women workers in the real sense of the word'. Recruitment was rapid. Muriel Heagney, a well-known trade union activist and feminist, became organiser of the AEU women's section. In May 1943, they produced a special recruitment pamphlet, and the first meeting of female shop stewards took place in Sydney in November 1943.[33]

Equal pay remained a central issue for tradesmen. While officials negotiated with the government, there were many stoppages on the shop floor. Engineers at the Ford factory in Homebush (Sydney) struck for three weeks in late 1942 over women employed on first class welding, and ACI Engineering saw a similar dispute. The strikes provided pressure for negotiations. Regulations introduced in May 1943 provided equal pay for tradesmen or second-class machinists, although male journeymen had preference. The pay question having been settled (from the men's point of view), the AEU became less concerned about female wages.[34]

The Sheet Metal Workers' Industrial Union (SMWIU) was very different. Much smaller and poorer before World War II, it didn't even have a publication until December 1936. The Victorian branch got its first typist and its first car in 1940. The union was small enough for the news-sheet to report the deaths of individual members. Sheet metal working only became a recognised apprenticeship in 1938, after many years of agitation.[35]

A small number of women had always worked in the industry, particularly making cans for food, but few state branches had tried to organise them before the war.

The SMWIU did not meet the massive influx in the first years of the war with the same resistance as the AEU, but the response to women in the industry and as members was still hesitant. Its 1940 federal conference attempted to restrict female labour to work on which they were engaged in 1930. In December 1941, the question of female labour was 'burning' in South Australia: 'Members must make up their minds as to the conditions under which they are prepared to tolerate this class of labour'. The participation of women members in industrial action over the dismissal of a Sydney delegate, their first association with a dispute, was met with mild surprise and condescension: 'We hasten to congratulate our "sisters" on their very fine show of solidarity'.[36]

Like the AEU, the SMWIU regarded the presence of large numbers of women as temporary. In April 1942, however, the union decided to organise them seriously. The news-sheet explained:

> It is more necessary than ever that they be recruited to the unions. Already the Ironworkers Union has thousands of female members and the ASE [Australasian Society of Engineers] has commenced to organise others. Shop stewards of the SMWIU where female labour is employed, must immediately organise them into our union, where they will receive the protection of our organisation and be able to play their part in the struggle to maintain and improve conditions.[37]

They appointed female shop stewards, held two conferences in 1943 and elected a women's committee. Miss Doris Beeby became women's organiser.

Before the establishment of the WEB, the SMWIU actually managed to get full equal pay for some jobs in munitions factories. They also achieved equal pay for junior females in several cases but were unable to get employers to apply it generally to adults.[38]

Under the WEB, the union changed its orientation slightly. Its General Secretary thought the *Women's Employment Act* was 'the most revolutionary legislation enacted for many years'. When the Board made a common ruling of 90 percent in the metal trades, although there were still applications for equal pay, their focus became implementation of the WEB ruling. The union's secretary reported in 1944 that the SMWIU made more applications to the WEB than any other union.[39]

The campaign seems to have been quite impressive. The union put up a 'strenuous' fight before the Board and called on the Labor Party after its election victory to use its majority in both houses to legislate for equal pay. They also pressured employers to improve the often scandalous conditions – such as poor ventilation, woefully inadequate toilets and washing facilities, heat and fumes. At one factory, the workers 'used to have to sit on the floor, but now we have tables and seats so are thankful for small mercies'. They backed their campaign up with calls for industrial action: 'We urge all our members…to keep up continuous agitation in their shops to secure improved conditions'. In Melbourne, fortnightly meetings were held at Trades Hall, and 'several women attended the meetings, mostly older women. They were very militant.'[40]

But the SMWIU's policy on the war was one of full support. Their continual push for higher production must have undermined industrial action. Such shop floor action as did occur was justified by arguments like: 'Workers…who get decent wages and conditions are going to be more efficient than those working under a sense of injustice.'[41] The first women's shop stewards' meeting in February 1943 pledged itself to 'avoid stoppages of work, which can only be harmful to the war effort.'[42] The second conference, in December, passed resolutions on:

> 100% unionism among women, closer co-operation between men and women workers in the workshops, carrying out of the Union's policy of full support for the war, with particular attention to combating absenteeism and lateness, to ensure increased production.[43]

This attitude was contradictory: the officials supported members when they struck but still tried to get them back to work as quickly as possible. In one case, the leadership recommended a return to work on the not very promising grounds that management proposed 'to confer with representatives of the unions involved and place the cards on the table'.[44] Nonetheless, the leader of the SMWIU, Tom Wright, was exceptional for his time. A member of the Central Committee of the Communist Party, Wright argued in the *Communist Review* that the party must support strikes if necessary 'to defend and extend wage increases won for women'.[45]

'Offending the public conscience': militancy during the war

Male unionists broadly accepted that industrial action should be curtailed. Restraint was based on political grounds, but there was also a material basis for it – for many men, at least. Although frozen, male wages were at a much higher level than during the Depression because of increased over-award payments, big increases in overtime at penalty rates, and 'war loadings'. Sydney newspapers advertised in 1941 for toolmakers at £12 ($24) a week (not including overtime), when the award rate was £6.11.0 ($13.10). Around this time, an adult woman in the metal trades with 12 months' experience (not doing tradesman's work) received £3.12 ($7.20), while a female worker under 16 got 12/6 ($1.25). Unsurprisingly, men thought that their own pay was fairly high, particularly compared to the prewar years, and they were often reasonably satisfied. When they were involved in struggles, these tended to be defensive, trying (as they saw it) to protect themselves against the new women workers. Moreover, men with a tradition of unionism were more tied to the officials: they were more inclined to follow the policies of the leadership, including support for the war effort.[46]

The situation for women was quite different. Their lack of an industrial tradition had the paradoxical effect that they were less likely to listen when union officials called for restraint. Moving from housework or traditional occupations into 'important' work for the first time, they gained new confidence. At the same time, the wage situation was chaotic.

At the beginning of the war, private industry was paying women 54 percent of the male rate. The Department of Munitions, under an agreement with the unions, paid 62 percent in its factories. The 1942 Metal Trades Award, set by the Arbitration Commission, awarded 65 percent for the first three months and 75 percent thereafter. The WEB rate was mostly 90 percent, except for tradesmen's work, which was 100 percent. In some workshops, there were two or three different pay rates for essentially the same work. In other cases, the company simply refused to pay the WEB rate and kept paying the lower rate of the Metal Trades

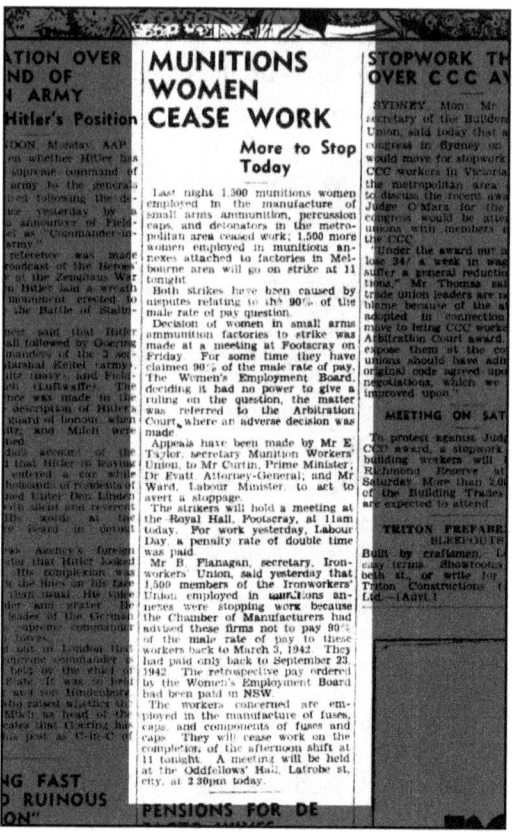

Award. Even government factories did this. In one case, where the AEU intervened, the workers received back pay totalling about $60,000 in value.[47]

The result was that women were often more militant than men, frequently undertaking industrial action, short stoppages and strikes. In fact, strikes by women workers at two private munitions factories in 1942 led to the establishment of the WEB itself. Between 1943 and 1945, Muriel Heagney recorded in her notebook many instances of stoppages over wage rates. In one dispute: 'girls on the comb benches threatened reduction in output on benches of 60 percent of the male output unless rates were equalized.'[48]

In the Small Arms Ammunition Factory in Footscray (Melbourne), there was a particular problem. As a prewar employer of women, the factory paid a lower rate than other munitions factories. Several thousand male and female workers held a stopwork meeting at the local band rotunda in early 1943, demanding the 90 percent rate for females. Then more than 2,000 women from government factories went on strike, without success.[49]

At Simmonds Aerocessories in South Melbourne, when workers were denied the WEB rates, 'feeling reached boiling point': 132 women sheet metal workers struck for the extraordinary period (especially in wartime) of over four months. With the strikers supported by 150 engineers, the case went as far as the High Court before the company capitulated and paid the 90 percent. The union officials supported the stand of the strikers, yet endeavoured: 'along with the shop committee, to try to come to satisfactory arrangements with the company to avoid any cessation of work'.[50]

When management at the electronics manufacturer AWA in Ashfield (Sydney) refused to pay the £5 ($10) granted by the WEB and kept wages at £3.12 ($7.20), 150 women and girls in the aircraft assembly section joined the AEU. When the Board arbitrarily decided that only 75 percent of them were entitled to the WEB rate, a three-week strike followed. Eventually, the members were 'prevailed upon' to return to work in return for the government undertaking legal proceedings. We are not told who did the prevailing, but we are left with a clear impression that the strikers were quite prepared to stay out longer.[51]

Direct action brought results more quickly than negotiations. When a Sydney company, Richard Hughes, refused to pay the WEB rate, the case dragged through the courts for over six months, with the company (backed by the industry association) repeatedly appealing to different bodies. By June 1944, it had become obvious to the workers that they were getting nowhere; a strike and lockout led quickly to a settlement involving the equivalent of $6,000 in back pay. In October 1942, 450 female employees from four other Sydney factories only needed to threaten to stop work for the employers to agree to give them retrospective pay.[52]

Daily stopwork meetings followed the failure of the employers at a Footscray (Melbourne) munitions factory to pay the awarded 90 percent. Jessie Street, a well-known feminist of the time, described the atmosphere at one meeting. The (male) secretary of the FIA assured them they would get their money and urged them to return to work for the sake of 'the boys in the trenches'. This provoked an angry response and shouts of 'We know all about the boys in the trenches...they're our husbands and sons'. A very militant meeting, followed by a strike, led Prime Minister Evatt to send a telegram promising to 'bring pressure to bear' if they went back to work, but the response was riotous. After three days of the strike, Evatt agreed to pay the difference until the employers paid the full 90 percent.[53]

Rosemary Davies, who worked in aircraft repair at Sydney airport, told how, when their 90 percent rate was cut, all the women joined the union and wanted action.[54] The union advised her to organise a stopwork:

All that night I wondered if the girls would do such an unusual thing (for them). All the papers and magazines told us that strikes and stopwork meetings were anti-war effort and quite taboo with the boys at the front. Next morning in the locker room, I...asked them to join me out on the tarmac at morning tea time for the stop work meeting... The men talked to the girls and encouraged them and some discussed whether to take action to support us.

On the tarmac, Rosemary climbed onto some wheeled aircraft-steps:

By then the girls had gathered courage and passed my prepared resolution unanimously, and became stirred up... They stubbornly refused to go back to work until Captain Young came to see them. The foreman carried the message to him, but he refused, saying he would accept a men's delegation. This made the girls mad!

After two hours, the men did see the boss, and the women's pay was restored at the next payday.

Even though the immediate claims were over wages, other issues contributed to the militancy. At Kavanagh and English in Sydney, where women sheet metal workers struck for over five weeks in 1943 over failure to pay the 90 percent, a union delegate had attacked the firm earlier in the year for refusing to do anything about conditions: 'The factory is in a very dirty condition and is infested with vermin... There are only three toilets for 75 girls.' During the strike, the *Sheet Metal Worker* reported that: 'there was widespread interest and support throughout the trade, and voluntary collections were made to supplement relief.' Eventually, the Trades and Labour Council intervened. With complete solidarity, the strikers won.[55]

The WEB rates only applied to about 85,000 women. The remainder of the 800,000 working during the war were in more traditional areas, where wages were already established and pegged at very low rates. In the metal industry, with overtime, pay could range up to £9 ($18) per week; but, in food processing, it would not have exceeded £4 ($8).[56] Unsurprisingly, there was a critical shortage of labour in the industries supplying the food, clothing and other supplies to the Australian and US forces (not to speak of the civilian population). In 1942, rather than raise wages, the authorities introduced a form of industrial conscription known as Manpower, requiring all females without children between the ages of 18 and 45 to register. This created a lot of resistance. When they called

Metal union will support strike by women

Any stoppage or strike by women metal workers to enforce payment of award rates will be backed by the Sheet Metal Workers' Union.

This assurance was given by union secretary Tom Wright yesterday to a meeting of women union members.

Another development among discontented women war-workers yesterday was the cessation of work in all Sydney woollen, worsted, and cotton textile mills—affecting about 8000 employees.

About 50 Sydney factories, which employ 1500 women sheet metal workers, were represented at an all-day conference of women members of the Sheet Metal Workers' Union.

It was the first time in the history of Australian metal trades that women shop delegates had held a conference.

Commenting on a refusal by some employers to pay women workers 90 per cent. of the male wage, as ruled by the Women's Employment Board, Union Secretary Wright said that about 20 factories had not yet adopted the board's decision.

"These 20 factories are still trying to find legal loopholes in the board's ruling in order to withhold higher wages," he said.

"Our union dislikes hold-ups in any factory, but where an employer opposes the board's decisions, direct action is the only solution."

The union would support any direct action the girls decided to take, he added.

Lockers, Footbaths

Union women's organiser, Miss Doris Beeby, outlined the new Federal Industrial Code, drafted by the Women's Employment Board.

The code's "minimum standard" requirements for factories include:—

● A dining-room large enough to accommodate all women employees, and furnished with tables and seats.

● A dressing-room with lockers for every woman.

● An adequate number of washbasins, with hot and cold water.

● Hot showers where there are more than 20 women employees.

● Provision of foot-baths.

● Provision of seats in workshops wherever a woman can do her work sitting down.

Tea Facilities

● At least one seat to every three women for use in slack periods.

● Morning and afternoon breaks of 10 minutes each, and facilities for making tea.

● Rest room, with lounge, for use of women not feeling well.

Miss Beeby said introduction of this code would cause a big change in factory conditions within the next few months.

The following resolution was passed: "This meeting of delegates, representing women employees of aircraft, sheet-metal working, and canister factories protests against the delay of those employers who have not yet obeyed the common rule decision of the Women's Employment Board.

"While pledging ourselves to avoid stoppages of work which can only be harmful to the war effort, we warn the employers concerned that there is a strong feeling amongst women employees about the delay, and that further delay will lead to serious disputes for which the employers will bear full responsibility."

A deputation from the Textile Workers' Union met Federal Labor Minister Ward yesterday.

Mr. Ward would make no comment later, but it is understood that the discussion pointed to a probable resumption of work after tomorrow's meetings.

The deputation to Mr. Ward followed

a union decision, as the result of which all employees in Sydney woollen, worsted, and cotton textile mills stopped work at 7.30 a.m. yesterday when night workers finished their shift.

These mills normally employ 8000 hands.

Most of the strikers are involved because key women workers walked out last week.

Stopwork meetings to deal with a strike involving 5000 workers (mostly women) have been arranged by the Textile Workers' Union at Leichhardt, Liverpool, and Parramatta at 10 a.m. tomorrow.

Meetings will also be held at Lithgow, Orange, Albury, and Goulburn. Mills in these centres employ about 1000 hands, and are not so far involved in the strike.

The strikers claim that the Arbitration Court has unduly delayed delivery of a judgment concerning claims for higher wages.

Union officials hope that at tomorrow's meetings strikers will decide to resume work immediately.

CHIEF PETTY-OFFICER LOTT and [...]

Pictures back in gallery

MELBOURNE, Sat.—Sixty paintings, worth £250,000, are to be re-hung by the Melbourne National Gallery.

They were stowed away a year ago because of the danger of air-raids. The paintings are the most valuable in the gallery's collection, and include the Van Eyck, valued at £63,000.

The paintings will be re-hung to enable the Americans to see them.

They include: Hans Memling's Pieta; a Flemish Triptych, and the Flemish 15th century Descent From The Cross.

SCHEHERAZADE OFFICER TO S[...]

A tiny portable radio Scheherazade is owned by Ch[...] on Allied serviceman.

"I call her Scheherazade because she talks to me every night when I go to bed," said Mr. Lott yesterday.

(Scheherazade was the wife of the Caliph Haroun-al-Raschid, who, in the "Arabian Nights," chose to tell her husband stories for a thousand and one nights in preference to having her head chopped off.)

Mr. Lott's Scheherazade is the size of a cigar box.

When folded together "she" can be carried like a minute suitcase, or even in a pocket.

"I have a lot of fun with her in restaurants," he said. "Sometimes I put her between two people who are having a meal, and they can't make out where the music is coming from.

"If I'm sitting in a tram, I set her [...]

14,923 bags of potatoes on way to end latest famine

Sydney's present potato famine should end tomorrow with the expected arrival of 14,923 bags of Tasmanian potatoes.

Deputy Potato Controller Squires said yesterday the shortage was due to a temporary seasonable lull.

Supplies had not been frozen to supply the Services, he added.

Manager of J. Fernandez, wholesalers (Mr. J. Dearman), said: "Fixed prices will give a monopoly to the big buyers. The small man will be squeezed out, and the public will be served up any rubbish.

"I think it's wrong to try to fix prices of perishable commodities."

Mr. Henry Woolfe, of Henry Woolfe Pty., said that when the wholesale prices became effective fish prices at his cafe in George Street would be correspondingly reduced.

Randwick storekeeper J. W. Power said yesterday he had refused to buy potatoes at £3 a bag (fixed price is 17/-).

New Fish Prices

The new fixed prices for fish imposed by Prices Commissioner Copland on Friday, are about 50 per cent. lower than the ruling market. They are not yet operating.

New ceiling prices a lb. for popular lines, with yesterday's market in brackets, are:—

Snapper, 1/2 (2/- to 2/9); whiting 1/4 (2/- to 2/6); bream, /10 (1/3 to 1/9); garfish, /4 to /10 (1/- to 1/3); flathead, /8 (formerly fixed at /9½); jewfish, /9 (1/9); mullet, /7 (formerly fixed at /9); kingfish, /7 (1/3).

President of the Master Fish Merchants' Association (retailers) George Freeman said agents had brought price fixation on themselves.

"They are already operating a racket," he said. "You rarely see flathead in a suburban shop. They all go [...]

This is hard to stomach

up 2,000 in Sydney to work in fruit-canning factories, 1,800 failed to attend the interview, while some who came brought borrowed babies to prove their unavailability. Manpower could also force transfers; Queensland munitions workers sometimes had 24 hours' notice to go to work in canneries. These women were hostile and, according to the FIA's paper *Labour News*, were being 'kept at work with difficulty'. Addressing strikers at Bulimba Cannery in 1944, the union officials successfully argued that striking was only 'a last resort'. The women returned to work in return for negotiations which brought only a small gain – an increase of 16s ($1.60) on their wage of £3 ($6) for that season only, and after that a drop back to £3.5.0 ($6.50).[57]

Anger at the Manpower regulations was one reason female union membership rose from 32.8 percent of the female workforce in 1939 to 51.9 percent in 1945; the number of disputes rose from 416 to 945.[58]

The textile industry saw important strikes during the war. In September 1941, mass stopworks in several Victorian centres led to 20,000 striking over war loadings:

> After the strike decision, about fifty men and women rushed the stage and tried to take over the meeting. They were quickly dispersed by the police. Speakers were howled down and counted out. Faction fights broke out in the audience. Women screamed at one another, and when the division...was carried by a large majority, calls of 'what about the boys overseas fighting for 5/- a day' 'scab' and 'Fascist' were heard above the din.[59]

Around the same time, 9,000 in Sydney defied their leadership in a strike. It started at Alexandria Spinning Mills, where bad conditions underlay the militancy. There was no lunchroom, and the workers 'used to get mad when they read about (the boss's) race horses winning'. Donations from unionists supported the strike, and shopkeepers gave food. Publicity included speaking from a stump in the Domain, and many young women 'came forward who'd never spoken in public before...they got a wonderful response and they were very good'.[60] After two weeks, the *Sydney Morning Herald* thundered: 'probably no strike since the war has so offended the public conscience'.[61]

Another major struggle in 1943 followed a failure to raise pay from the traditional 54 percent in a new award. Again at Alexandria Spinning Mills, 1,000 women 'stormed out' of their factory, set up a strike committee, picketed and sent delegations to other factories. At one, 'the striking girls scaled wire grilles

to reach the girls working inside... At other factories the girls were confronted by police at the factory gates.' By the end of the week, rank and file committees were leading 10,000 workers, who wanted a 'continuation of their struggle until they had received some kind of justice.'[62]

They would need all their strength. Arrayed against them were the employers, the Arbitration Court, the Labor government and the press. Textile Workers' Union officials were openly hostile. Not only did they direct the workers to return to work; they gave strikers' names to the Arbitration Court so that they could be fined for 'absenteeism'. They also manoeuvred so that all workers in the industry could vote on a continuation, rather than just the strikers.⁶³

Among those pressuring for a return to work was the Communist Party, which supported the war effort on orders from Moscow. Betty Reilly, a CPA activist who worked in a mill, described the response when the strikers' delegation arrived to call them out:

> Due mainly to my influence, 'Winnie the War Winners' were in the majority at the AWM [Australian Woollen Mills] and my workmates shouted back 'what about the war effort' and continued to work.⁶⁴

However, when Reilly later spoke at a mass meeting, the response was very different:

> I got up and...tried to convince them of the need to keep on producing for the war effort... Well this was greeted with howls of derision.⁶⁵

> I'd be the only woman on record who took the count at the Leichhardt Stadium for proposing to hundreds of irate workers that we return to work in the interests of defeating fascism.⁶⁶

Although Reilly and others like her sincerely supported workers' struggles, the party's position posed a contradiction for them. She herself later recognised:

> I should have been on the side of those women, criticising the lax and complacent union officials, who, rather than lead us in this strike...were forcing us back to work.[67]

There were strikes in several other industries. In 1941, the government tried to ban the Christmas holidays. Large numbers of workers, many of whom had worked overtime for the past year, defied the ban without official union sanction and resigned on Christmas Eve, only to reapply for their old jobs early in January. Because boot and food factories were mainly involved, many must have been women.[68]

Betty Reilly c 1950s

REBEL WOMEN

The CTU had a policy of no strikes during wartime. A statement from the leadership claimed that:

> in so far as the men were concerned, this objective was largely achieved and at no stage during the war was there a dispute even of a minor nature involving males [but]... Circumstances in regard to female employment are totally at variance to those surrounding employment of males and the result has been somewhat disastrous.[69]

Perhaps this referred to Berlei, where the CTU was hand-in-glove with the management. There was no shop floor organisation. Workers were angered by the sacking of a popular manager and the storing of materials in their lunch-room. Most workers were young and not long out of school; lacking knowledge of industrial traditions, they used a technique from school, passing notes from machine to machine. In this way, they elected representatives and decided to stop work after lunch. As part of the settlement, management agreed to a social committee. The bosses' attempt to dictate the committee's membership was foiled when workers elected committee members, again by notes.[70]

When the WEB awarded female railway employees 90 percent in January 1943, rejecting union calls for equal pay, angry Melbourne porters and ticket collectors marched from Flinders and Spencer Street stations to a protest meeting in the middle of peak hour traffic. Waitresses at restaurants at Farmers Department Store in Sydney struck for several weeks in the same year over the sacking of a waitress and the issue of holiday pay.[71]

Towards the end of the war, industrial disputation stepped up. Daphne Gollan explained: 'workers' war weariness and frustration at long hours, pegged wages and bad working conditions in some industries made them very ready to strike.'[72]

> New South Wales, during the 20 months ending August 31 [1944], had 1,432 industrial disputes involving 588,951 workers and resulting in a loss of 1,461,671 man-days. At times in that period and since, industrial disputes wholly or partially deprived the neutral citizen of meat, bread, laundry, newspapers, tyres, theatrical entertainment, hospital attention, buses and trams, coke for stoves, potatoes, restaurants, hot baths, country and interstate travel and other amenities.[73]

These included lost 'woman-days'. For example, about 450 waitresses working mainly at Sargents and Cahills restaurants in Sydney took industrial action in

September 1944. They decided not to work on Fridays and Saturdays as a protest against the employers' refusal to implement a new award.[74] Women and girls at the *Sun* sparked off the 1944 Sydney printing strike. Although they were poorly paid, the issue was not wages but having to work a 44-hour week while male compositors worked 40 hours. Females were new in this industry and had already made their mark: 'Lots of old customs got tossed overboard, due to the girls.' The union officials were largely uninterested, not even including their names on published membership lists. It was only a week after the strike began that the federal secretary realised that they worked 44 hours.[75]

A little war job

In wartime, the argument that all classes and layers in society have the same interests is particularly strong. With the 'national interest' foremost in most people's minds, the idea that all were essentially in the same boat was very appealing. Yet, a glance at the experiences of upper-class women shows that they lived through a very different war from that experienced by the working class.

Early in the war, voluntary work played a major role in creating what Carmel Shute describes as: 'a mass war consciousness amongst women which transcended class barriers and provided a persuasive model of self-sacrifice.'[76] In addition, it undermined the bargaining power of those moving into the new industry sectors. 'Voluntarism branded women's labour as cheap – and expendable.' This was an important factor in forcing unions to accept dilution.

While voluntary work was advocated for all, it was only practical for those with leisure and independent incomes. The executive members of the Women's Voluntary National Registry in NSW all lived in exclusive Sydney suburbs. They had backgrounds in conservative women's organisations; several had honours; and at least two held the title of 'Lady'. While ostensibly open to all, most women's service organisations used economic means to restrict their membership. Members had to pay for expensive uniforms and, in some cases, for their own cars, motorcycles, horses or rifles. Muriel Heagney denounced the Voluntary Aid Society as a 'socialite outfit' and claimed that experienced clerks, nurses, domestics and cooks were being rejected because of a preference for 'dilettantes'.

Many continued their usual social round, disguised as patriotic activities. A writer to the *Women's Weekly* objected to those 'who play their bridge so many days a week, *and not in the cause of some war charity* [italics added]'. The Ladies' War Aid Kennel Association gathered 'to conduct dog parades and other activities in aid of patriotic funds', holding its first champion-dog show at the elegant

Toorak residence of Mrs G. J. Coles – who 'as usual came forward and lent her spacious grounds'. Mrs A. B. Challen insisted that 'croquet now is only a means of keeping players fit for useful war work.'

The most popular courses for the socialites were in driver training. Some did do real work – of a sort. Labor MP Eddie Ward drew attention to 'well known Melbourne society girls' working in the Department of Information. This was defended as voluntary and 'a little war job'; the Minister denied that they were driven to the offices in limousines. Some even went into factories. Dame Mabel Brookes worked at an explosives plant at a time when many factories were still working a 56-hour week, or more with overtime. She used to:

> turn up regularly in her Rolls Royce about three days a week. She'd be there from about 10.00 am to 3.00 pm. Everyone fussed around her and she didn't work very hard, but she wasn't such a bad stick.[77]

Unions made some effort to resist. The Council of Action for Equal Pay kept a close watch on the women's auxiliaries and volunteers whose work 'tended to undermine the campaign for equal pay'. At a conference in 1940, delegates criticised the government for emphasising *unpaid* industrial work while 'ignoring the new special problems inherent in the socially necessary *paid* work of women and youths in wartime'. One delegate warned that voluntary labour could be used to break strikes. Carmel Shute comments:

> The voluntary war organisations remained outside the sphere of trade union organisation and their free labour undercut, largely indirectly, the wages and conditions of workers of both sexes. Moreover, their notion that the primary duty of women in the war was to serve the 'national cause', irrespective of the conditions under which they did so, seriously diminished the bargaining power of women as they entered new sectors of industry and the armed services.[78]

The role of socialites can be seen in the 1943 strike at Duly and Hansford in Marrickville (Sydney).[79] In May, 1,000 munitions workers, mostly women, struck for 10 weeks against the employment of non-unionists. The management was anti-union, and the workers already had some experience of short stoppages when first the FIA and ASE members, and then the whole workplace, stopped over 10 workers who refused to join. Despite government pressure and a hostile press, the strikers won.

MONDAY DAILY TELEGRAPH JULY 19, 1943

WOMEN BITTER ABOUT STRIKERS

Soldier Calls War Workers' Stand Against Union "Tobruk Of Industrial Front"

Some of the non-unionists who have been forced to leave Duly and Hansford's munition annexe strongly criticised the unions and the management yesterday.

If the strike committee is assured today by the management that the 10 non-unionists have left the job, it will direct the strikers at a subsequent mass meeting to report for work.

A general resumption of work in the main factory is expected by Wednesday or Thursday.

MISS E. PEACOCK (non-unionist, who opposes strikes).

"... I'm ashamed to be an Australian, and I never want to do another thing to help the war effort."

Wanted Every Chance For Son

A soldier in New Guinea has called the dispute "The Tobruk of the Industrial Front."

He is the son of Mrs. Frank Howell, Ramsgate Avenue, Bondi, one of the 10 non-unionists who have lost their jobs.

The management of Duly and Hansford on Friday informed its non-unionists that the annexe where they worked would be closed.

The strike began on May 3, when 10 non-unionists, nine of them women, refused to take an illegal holiday in lieu of Anzac Day.

Since then more than 1050 employees have been on strike and 339,000 manhours lost in essential war work.

Mrs. Howell said yesterday:

"I took up munition work because I wanted my son to have every chance. I've kept up this fight because he wanted me to.

"He and his soldier pals told us to stick to our guns." Ken also said he would like to give the unionists a burst from his Owen gun.

"He was furious, and made me send him all the newspaper cuttings."

Won't Stay Home

"If Mr. Curtin thinks I'm going to stay at home just because we've been forced to ask for our release at Duly and Hansford's, he's mistaken.

"I'm taking two weeks' holiday, then I'm going to find another job in a non-unionist factory. I've been doing munition work for 17 months now, and it will take more than a few unionists to stop me from keeping it up.

"It was the firm that gave up the fight—not us! They were frightened the Government would divert some of their biggest orders to other factories. We had no intention of quitting."

Mrs. Howell said that an Ironworkers' Union official had followed her home one night, had waylaid her in a dark alley, and tried to force her to join the union.

Other unionists had jeered at her and hooted her in trams, trains, and at the factory, and told her she was letting down the boys at the front.

Mrs. Howell said that Mrs. J. E. Cassidy, a fellow non-unionist, had received up to 100 letters from servicemen and civilians telling her not to give in.

Other non-unionists interviewed yesterday were indignant and shocked.

Miss Jean Duncan, Fotheringham Street, Marrickville, said:—

"I intend to do anything while the unpleasantness I should just carry on with my work.

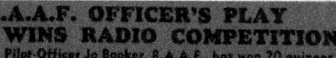

Miss Jean Duncan

"Once alone then I offered to leave, but was told it would not be advisable. I feel that the firm should have stuck to their original attitude.

"I had never seen the inside of a factory before, but after the first few weeks I loved the job.

"Sometimes I used to feel I just can't get up today, I'm too tired. Then I'd remember that the boys at the front could never be too tired for their job and up I'd get.

"I felt that women like myself, with no real ties, should go into a factory. I gave up living at Double Bay and came out here to Marrickville to live in this war while I was told it was better to remain.

"It came as a great shock to realise that the employers were not going to stand by us.

"This strike need never have started. I've been doing this work for two years, and before I started I was told that it was not a union shop and that I need not join unless I wished.

"In peacetime I think that unions are a necessary evil, but in wartime the whole country should be on the same footing as the fighting forces, and subject to the same discipline.

"I would be quite willing to work for a soldier's pay. What we need in this country is a few bombs to make people realise there is a war on."

Miss Elisabeth Peacock, of Greenbank Street, Marrickville, said:

"I am ashamed of being an Australian. I never want to do another thing to help the war effort.

"When I think that two of the men of my family have died for this country, I can only thank God they didn't die on Australian soil.

"The week before the strike, I went to the office and saw Mr. Hansford. I said that if I did not want to cause trouble for the firm, and asked if they would prefer to give me my clearance.

"Mr. Hansford said if I could stand the unpleasantness I should just carry on with my work.

Public Wanted Legal Action

Fifty-one per cent. of people questioned in a Daily Telegraph survey during the last week said that they believed the Government should have applied the law against strikes in protected industries to the strikers at Duly and Hansford's.

A representative cross-section of the people was asked:—

"Do you or do you not consider that the Federal Government should have applied at Duly and Hansford's the law which makes strikes in protected industries illegal?"

ANSWERS:—

Yes: 51 per cent.

No: 31 per cent.

Undecided: 18 per cent.

Of the men questioned, 47 per cent. answered "Yes" and 40 per cent. "No"; 13 per cent. were undecided.

Of the women questioned, 55 per cent. answered "Yes" and 20 per cent. "No"; 25 per cent. were undecided.

"Will Cost Votes"

"I'm going in on Monday—the firm has not given us our clearances yet.

"We were not very many to stand up against the unions and the Government. But this fight will have to be fought again—and it will be a bigger fight next time.

"The Government will lose votes over this. Every thinking citizen knows that strikes simply won't do in wartime."

Miss Veronica McGrane, also of Greenbank Street, Marrickville, said:—

Miss Veronica McGrane

"I don't quite know what I'm going to do yet. The strain has been terrible.

"But if it came to going it all over again for my country, I'd do it willingly.

"I used to feel pretty awful going past these pickets, but the thing that hurts most is the fact that our employers hadn't the courage to come and face us.

"They should have stuck to their principles, instead of trying to remain neutral.

"I only hope there will be a few more who will stand up and do what we have tried to do.

"Yes, I'd still go back if I thought it would do any good."

Mr. O. M. McDonald, secretary of the Metal Trades Employers' Association, said last night that the works were to be reopened to "enable important war production to proceed."

Production was to proceed, he added, after the people had been provided with indisputable evidence of the Curtin Government's complete incapacity to discipline law-breakers.

"The hold-up of war production at Duly and Hansford's works occurred not because of any dispute with the employers, but because a few men and women had the courage to stand up for the principles of freedom and loyalty to Government laws."

R.A.A.F. OFFICER'S PLAY WINS RADIO COMPETITION

Pilot-Officer Jo Booker, R.A.A.F., has won 20 guineas for his play, "Slit Trench."

It has been chosen from 75 plays as the winning entry in the Australian Broadcasting Commission's play competition for servicemen.

"Slit Trench" was broadcast last night on 2FC.

MRS. FRANK HOWELL.

"... If Mr. Curtin thinks I'm going to stay at home because the munition annexe where I worked has closed down he's mistaken."

Duly and Hansford strike Marrickville (Sydney) over employment of non-unionists May 1943

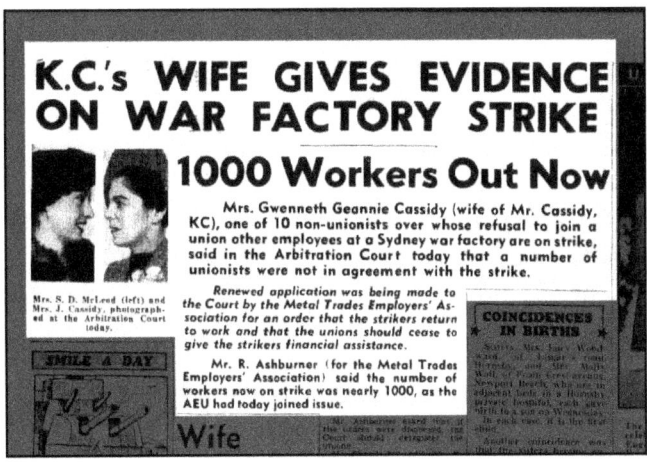

One of the non-unionists, Mrs G. Cassidy, was the socially prominent wife of a KC who hoped that the fight at Duly and Hansford would be a first step in eliminating strikes. The (upper) class arrogance of another can be seen from her comments after meeting a representative of the Minister for Labour: 'It is unfortunate they sent that type of man to interview us. All the time they have treated us like wharf labourers'. Daphne Gollan notes that the non-unionists combined ostentatious dedication to the war effort with: 'resentment at workers' efforts to use labour's favourable bargaining position to gain some advantage'.

It is fashionable to give all credit for the equal pay fight to feminists and to place the blame for failure to achieve it during the war on union sexism. Andree Wright cites Jessie Street's belief that: 'half hearted support from the trade unions was largely responsible' and argues that more could have been achieved 'had ACTU co-operation been more frequent'.[80]

In fact, feminists also played a role in restricting wage gains. Jessie Street herself was a leader in the conservative United Associations of Women, whose membership was mostly well to do. During the 1940 basic wage case, this organisation attempted to intervene to put their case for a gradual introduction of equal pay, with 60 percent immediately and 5 percent quarterly increments. The unions were furious, because they had been arguing for full equal pay; but the publicity for a gradual approach weakened their case. The United Associations of Women's class-based concern for the ability of employers to pay outweighed their support for equal rights.[81]

In any case, we shouldn't focus entirely on union *officials*, when rank and file action achieved so much. Ryan and Rowse comment: 'it is difficult to gain an accurate picture of the class-consciousness of the women in the workforce'.[82]

Even Daphne Gollan, in her study of a dispute, says: 'the main actors, the women strikers, remain silent and invisible.'[83] Yet, this chapter has shown that the curtain of silent invisibility is not so difficult to lift. We have found a picture of repeated industrial struggle.

Even a 'national cause' as intense as the war could not abolish the class divisions affecting both genders. As working women faced new difficulties in the postwar era, a class conflict would again shape their lives.

UAW equal pay demonstration early 1960s.

Against the stream
Women and the left, 1945-1968

TOM O'LINCOLN

Last year saw the publication of *Women in Australia*, a sociological treatise by Norman MacKenzie... Barely any mention is made of the trade union women's committees. Norman MacKenzie has written about us at length, reduced us to statistics, commented on our way of life but he does not understand that it is such organisations of the working class which will play a decisive part in our future.[1]

—*Our Women*, 1963

MacKenzie's book is not the only example of neglect. The two decades after World War II have received little attention from students of women's history – probably because it was a time of defeat. What lessons can be learned, after all, from a time when women were 'sent back into the home', and conservative social roles became predominant?

Yet, defeat is never absolute. In reality, women were not sent back into the home at all. After a temporary dip right after the war, their numbers in the civilian workforce began to rise again and rapidly exceeded the highest wartime levels. The *ideology* which taught that their place was in the home did assist the employers in cutting back their wages and conditions. Even so, there were numerous struggles in the late 1940s through the 1950s that limited the Cold War right-wing onslaught and helped lay the basis for a new radicalisation in the 1960s. During this time, the task of keeping the idea of women's equality alive fell largely to the political left, especially the Communist Party and its allies.

The CPA acted within a political framework that was, in some ways, quite conservative. While the Bolshevik revolution had taken radical measures in the

THESE six girls are Queens of Committees working in s From left: MISS SOCIALISM (Vera Pearce, Batman c South Port), MISS EQUAL PAY (Ila Spicer, Bourke), M THE PEOPLE (Margery Stevens, Eastern), MISS HIGHER

Note well-known author Wendy Lowenstein second from left.

areas of sexuality, abortion and family relations, the rising Stalinist bureaucracy had, from the late 1920s onwards, reinstated the family as a sacred institution, banned abortion and imposed sexual puritanism. These policies found their reflections in the Western communist parties, which also saw the family as a bastion of socialism and built much of their work among women around traditional conceptions of the female role.

During the 1930s, this tendency was still counterbalanced by a strong emphasis on women in the workplace, as Chapter 3 illustrates. Even after the war, communists still argued for bringing women into production, and organising them there, as a prerequisite for emancipation. In practice, however, the emphasis was increasingly on housewives. Betty Reilly's report to the 1948 Party Congress announced: 'A broad people's movement must include all progressive sections of women, particularly working class housewives and women from industry' and claimed that: 'the conditions are maturing in the localities and the factories.'[2] The order of priority is clear enough.

...districts for the Communist Party's 1948 Christmas Fair. ...ct), MISS NEW DEAL FOR YOUTH (Wendy Lowenstein, ...PEACE (Betty Games, Southern), MISS HOMES FOR ...SIC WAGE (Val Carmichael, Footscray-Williamstown).

Therefore, the party was by no means a model force for women's liberation. However, in a highly conservative society, it was the most advanced political movement of any size – and one with significant roots in the working class. Sometimes, the communists made comments prefiguring the cultural critiques later made by women's liberation, as when Freda Brown wrote in 1964: 'changing fashions are not dictated by women's desires, comfort or climate.'[3] If their achievements were modest, that partly reflects the difficult conditions of the time. This chapter differs from all the others in that it offers no remarkable examples of women taking the lead in big struggles. Such developments are much less likely in times of reaction. It does, however, relate a number of smaller struggles which kept some idea of women's rights alive.

After the war

Well before the war ended, there was talk of women eventually surrendering their jobs to men. These ideological pressures mounted as time went on. The unions were by no means immune. In 1943, the SMWIU insisted:

We must remain united. Not preference for one against another, but work or full maintenance for all must be our slogan for the post war period.

Only a year later, the same union signed an agreement with AWA in 1944 over postwar retrenchments. Preference was to be given to men and boys, particularly where the women were on the (higher) WEB rates. In February 1945, the union's news-sheet published a cartoon showing a woman in overalls watching her husband shave. 'Jealous?' he says. The SMWIU still had 15 percent female membership at this stage.[4]

Yet, there were many cases where men stood up for women's right to work. Jessie Street describes an example of a Sydney factory where eight women remained after the war, still on equal pay. When management tried to cut their pay, the men threatened to strike. When the company then dismissed the women, saying that it would employ only males, the men struck until the women were reinstated.[5]

The late 1940s and early 1950s brought attacks on the higher wages and access to jobs that women had won during the war. In 1949, the employers took a test case to the High Court and secured a decision invalidating the WEB regulations; pay for females was now to be set at only 75 percent of the male rate. The bosses then carried the attack into the arbitration machinery. In March 1951, Conciliation Commissioner Galvin also endorsed the 75 percent figure.

During these years, employers also took the offensive on the job. There, however, they often met fierce resistance. In November 1948, women at Thompson and Scougall's, Alexandria (Sydney) won a wage rise after a strike threat. In May 1950, 32 men and eight women struck together for equal pay at Claude Neon, also in Sydney. Six months later, female postal workers forestalled a federal government attempt to abolish equal pay by threatening industrial action.

Members of the New Housewives Association march Melbourne 1949, Alma Morton in the lead. Slogans were painted on aprons due to the ban on political placards. Referring to Premier Thomas Hollway they read: 'New Housewives have had hopeless Hollway' and 'Tom says price control can go. Tom can go'. Participants had to remove the aprons before being allowed into Parliament House.

Members of the Miners' Women's Auxiliary holding thank you sign from striking coal miners. Probably from the Great Greta or Glen Davis sit ins (known as 'stay-puts') NSW 1952. (Noel Butlin Archives Centre, Australian National University).

February 1951 saw a two-and-a-half week stoppage at half-a-dozen Sydney metal shops, successfully defending wartime pay rates; April of the same year witnessed ironworkers in Newcastle on strike over the same issue; and July saw female meatworkers at Swifts in Brisbane successfully stop attempts to push their pay down to 66 percent of the male rate. These actions all occurred in industries with a significant CPA presence and reflected the presence of a left-wing political leadership. However, it appears that there was a much more widespread discontent among female workers at the time: the *Communist Review* reported a case at Dunlop's Weatherproof factory in Wagga Wagga:

> women workers…completely unorganised, rose in protest at the placing of men at double their pay rates, at the same tables. The inequality was too obvious, the men had to be given different work.[6]

Neither labour historians nor feminist writers have covered these events; I learned about them from reading the communist press of the time. The most impressive action, reported by the party paper *Queensland Guardian*, was at Rheem in Brisbane. Management cut pay for females from 90 percent of the male rate to just over 75 percent. On 11 April 1951, the women – including a number of migrant workers (at that time widely considered to be incapable of militancy) – struck. The communist-led SMWIU backed the strike. Within a fortnight, around 100 men had come out in support of the 23 women, who were themselves busily engaged in addressing shop floor meetings around Brisbane. One of them told engineering workers at Evans Deakin: 'We're doing the same work as men, yet we've had a big cut in our pay. The men support us because it's an unjust attack.'[7]

After three months, the strikers settled for 87 percent of the male rate, equivalent to 90 percent of what the male rate had been when the dispute began.

During the immediate postwar years, the CPA was also heavily involved with housewives. Having previously worked within the conservative Housewives' Association (as well as the Country Women's Association), in 1948 it led a breakaway to form a New Housewives' Association (NHA). The communist press claimed 50 branches and a membership of 3,000 for it in NSW. In Melbourne, a member of the rival Association conceded that the breakaway group began life with branches in 32 suburbs.[8]

Runaway inflation, lack of child care and the absence of even minimal amenities and services in the new working-class suburbs had produced a ferment among women after the war. The NHA was intended to be a 'mass organisation', organising around immediate issues and attempting to radicalise large numbers. This sometimes meant a low political level, with the NHA taking up glove making and flower arranging. On the other hand, there were some extremely militant actions. NHA members addressed factory meetings on issues concerning women and general politics. In Sydney, a group of them stormed into the gas company, to protest against rising charges, and were able to force the manager to see them. In Melbourne, 100 housewives marched into the Prices Branch office, demanding controls on meat prices.

The agitation around price inflation reached its peak in mass demonstrations in Sydney in 1948. The party paper *Tribune* claimed that the crowd numbered 10,000, reporting that the police had called it the biggest demonstration ever held in Sydney (hardly true). It won support as far away as Melbourne, where building workers at Moorabbin held a one-hour stoppage to coincide with it.[9]

The *Communist Review* hailed the success of the demonstration as indicating the 'beginnings of a People's Movement'. Unfortunately, this was not at all true. The large numbers were achieved partly by calling out the waterside workers, not by mobilising 10,000 housewives. Such methods were artificial and could not be repeated without exhausting the patience of the wharfies. The mass demonstration marked the peak, not the beginning, of the movement.[10]

Another important issue for the NHA was child care, a pressing issue amidst the postwar 'baby boom'. It was a good issue to fight around; but here the party's family orientation betrayed its limitations. The agitation was not directed at state and federal governments, which had resources to fund child care on a large scale. Rather, there was a community orientation. At its worst, this seems to have amounted to self-help, with the party encouraging women to: 'help with functions to raise funds for the local kindergarten...or work with some form of housewives' association to improve conditions in the home.' At its best, the NHA sought to achieve its aims through local councils; but Daphne Gollan later recalled:

Women of Hunter Valley coal mining communities, wives of striking miners, protesting against mine closures 1957. These women had been ejected from their homes, which were owned by the mining company.

Newcastle Waterside Workers Federation Women's Strike Committee, 1956, distributed donated food to striking families, among other activities.

It was dreadfully difficult because the municipal councils didn't have the money... A very handsome day nursery was set up in, of all places, Double Bay [an affluent suburb]. A beautiful day nursery, but whether they needed it, of course...[11]

The NHA conducted various other activities, from cottage lectures to marketing wholesale fruit and vegetables. While the work sometimes lacked political direction, it offered some potential for winning support among larger numbers of working women. After 1949, however, as the party began suffering major defeats, it was abandoned.

The CPA also devoted considerable attention to organising the wives of male trade unionists. There was already a strong tradition of women's auxiliaries in the coalfields, and the communists sought to extend this to other industries in the postwar period.

The first auxiliary among seamen's wives arose in Sydney during World War II, and they became a general feature after the war. Similar groups were set up at various times in the building industry, in the metal trades and on the waterfront. Considering that the term 'auxiliary' carried implications of making tea rather than class struggle, the party encouraged them to call themselves 'women's committees'. Changing the terminology did not, in itself, ensure that the groups transcended wives' traditional role as 'hewers of cake and drawers of tea'. A 1963 article explained the aims and activities of the committees as:

> to explain to women the industrial and political demands of their menfolk so that women can take part in struggles fully understanding the issues involved. However, this is by no means their only function. The women meet socially, visit sick members, collect funds, run children's Christmas parties, celebrate International Women's Day, participate in May Day, assist other women's organisations with similar aims and play a vital part in the fight for peace.[12]

The social activities had more political importance than it might appear. Wives of seamen often led lonely lives, and ensuring the companionship of other women could be important, especially if they fell ill. The fact that a body linked to the union concerned itself with this built support for trade unionism. Even the tea making, by getting women together, could provide the beginnings of more ambitious ventures.

Doris Maxwell, a foundation member of the Waterside Workers' women's committee, explained that the union had first agreed to the committee 'mainly to assist in the union canteen', but by 1953 it took a step beyond that by sending some members along on a deputation to Canberra.

> By 1954 the women and the union felt it was time for us to get out of the canteen and take up wider activities. In the strike of November 1954, we were more than an auxiliary, and in the big strike of February this year [1956] we played a really important role.

In Brisbane, a committee representative joined the strike committee. One of the union officials, Matt Monroe, commented that: 'our members have had to be won to the idea of any committees of women' but 'now our committee and our members' wives are invited to our stopworks'. Similarly, in the Brisbane metal trades, strikers' wives attended a mass meeting and joined a union rally during a 1960 strike at Commonwealth Engineering Works.[13]

The committees often tried to familiarise wives with the workplace as well as the union. In Townsville in 1958, the local engineering union organiser conducted a tour of the powerhouse. In NSW, the committee associated with a building union 'developed the splendid idea of job excursions by women and children, to see their menfolk at work'. Sometimes more than sightseeing was involved: in 1962, women's committee members went out with organisers to address site meetings on issues surrounding that year's federal election.[14]

The Union of Australian Women

As the Cold War intensified, the communists and their allies retreated from the comparatively militant New Housewives to a broader, more moderate organisation.

The Union of Australian Women (UAW) was formed in 1950 and 1951. Its founders modelled it on European groups like the Union of Italian Women, which had arisen on an antifascist and antiwar program, then broadened its interests. Information about the European groups appears to have reached Australia through the international peace movement, and leading antiwar activists were involved in setting up the UAW. After 1956, they established a national structure and began publishing the magazine *Our Women*, whose circulation peaked at 10,000.

Some UAW activists have been at pains to insist that their organisation had no party affiliation. One of them told me:

UAW demonstration 1950s, probably Canberra

UAW demonstration over maternity allowance 1950s

As soon as it was set up, it was immediately attacked, as everything progressive was attacked, with the red bogey. So we had a hard row to hoe from the word go, and some people did drop out, once these rumours went around that it was a Communist front. So we've always stood on the ground that we were political but we were non-party, and any woman of the party had the right to come in, as long as they were prepared to work for peace, for women's rights, equal pay, children and development and education.[15]

There were indeed UAW branches with very few communists, and the group embraced a wide range of people. On the other hand, Pat Elphinston – who, as the organisation's first national secretary, was in a position to know – remarked in 1980 that the Sydney management committee had been 'loaded with Communist women'. At the top levels, the CPA set the tone. UAW policies were always compatible with those of the party, and the group has to be seen as part of the CPA strategy of building a broad 'people's front'.[16]

This was actually not a very radical strategy, and the UAW was not a very radical movement. Although the conditions under which the group operated were certainly difficult, it did not need to retreat as much as it did from an orientation to the workplace and class struggle. By 1948, women's employment levels had returned to their wartime peak. Their labour force participation rate rose throughout the 1950s, with married females especially moving into the workforce. The latter were more confident and assertive, perhaps because they were somewhat older. Being less likely to see themselves as just waiting to get married, they tended to take long-term union issues more seriously. It was possible to sow some militant seeds among them, as CPA member Stella Nord learned from practical experience.

New Housewives Association flyer about price rises.

After getting a job at the Swifts meat packing plant in Brisbane, Nord was able to emerge gradually as an agitator. In addition to her own efforts, this success owed something to the arrival of more married women, which improved the climate in the plant. It also owed something to the support she received from the CPA. She began by encouraging other women to demand (and win) a mirror in the dressing room – a small victory that laid the basis for bigger ones:

> It was essential, I felt, that the women themselves got their own confidence to front up to the [union] delegate and the boss and feel their own power.

She helped create a strong militant union consciousness by seeking their ideas for articles to appear in the communist job sheet; insisting that some union meetings be held in the women's dining room; then building a stoppage over uniforms:

> From these struggles there developed a new power relation situation, where the women themselves [were] all sticking together, while some of the men who were good lined up with the women, [and some other men] supported the boss. It became a clear demarcation of women plus militant workers opposed to the boss.[17]

It is likely that CPA women could have achieved more such successes with a stronger workplace orientation. Certainly, veteran communist Alice Hughes thought so, remarking later that, when the UAW was formed, the party should have argued the need to:

> go and work in industry, on the job ...[instead] I can remember having meetings in localities and trying to develop interest groups on the basis of craft work that I absolutely detested...when I should have been working in industry.[18]

Whatever its faults, however, the UAW was easily the most radical and class-conscious group of people working in the field of women's rights.

The UAW devoted a lot of attention to equal pay and deserves much of the credit for keeping this issue alive during the 1950s and early 1960s. *Our Women* carried a steady stream of articles on the subject, addressing the question of whether equal wages would mean the sack for female employees and reporting

UAW demonstration over equal pay walking on footpaths in city streets and ending at Parliament House, Melbourne early 1960s.

WOMEN
ARE AS SKILFUL
AS MEN
WHY NOT
THE SAME
PAY?

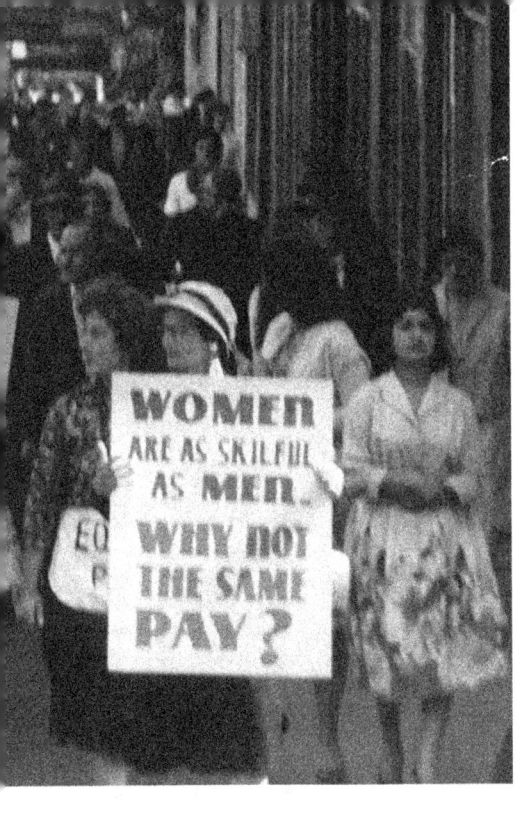

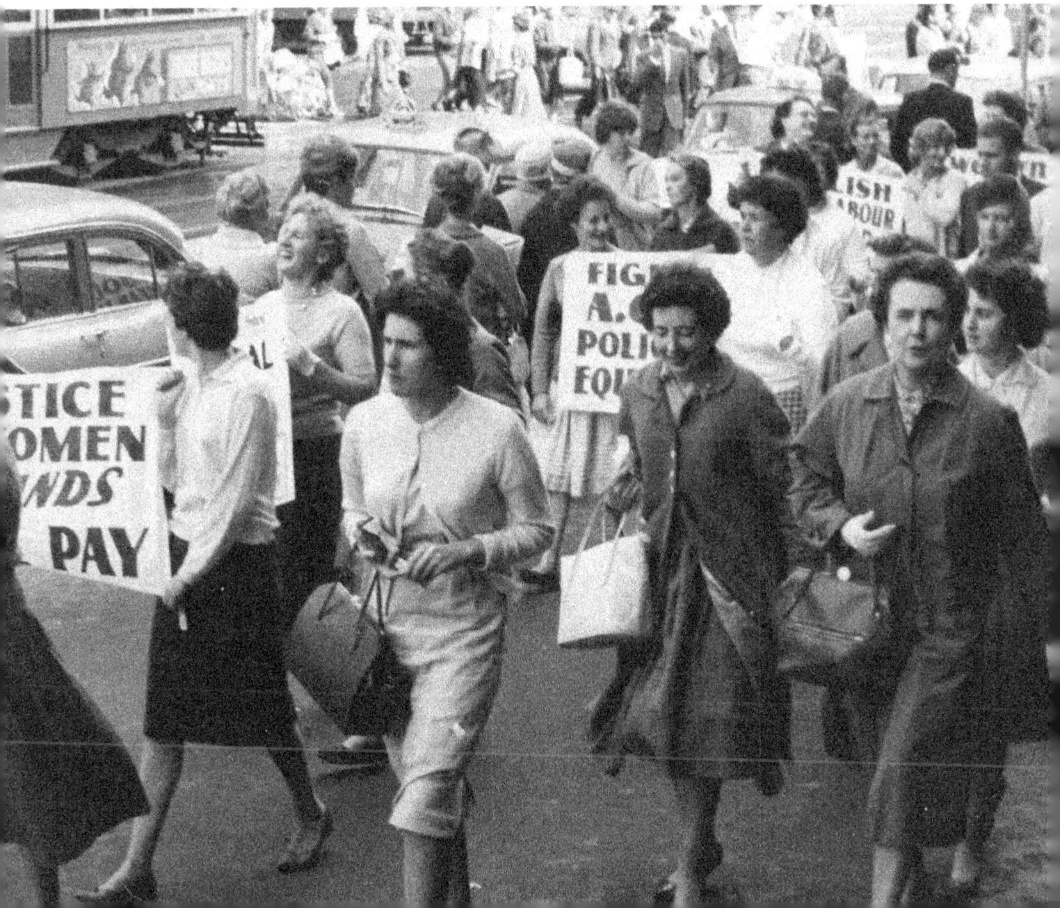
PAY

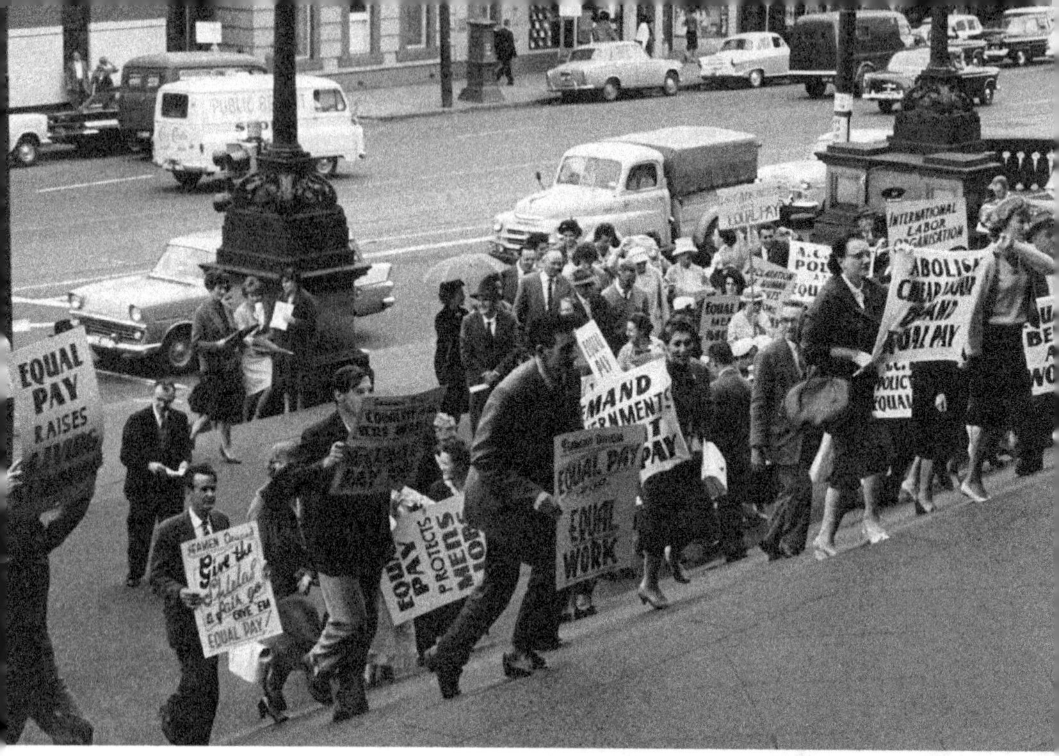
EQUAL PAY RAISES
INTERNATIONAL LABOR ORGANISATION
EQUAL PAY
Give the Sheilas a fair go GIVE 'EM EQUAL PAY!
PAY PROTECTS
EQUAL PAY
EQUAL WORK

A.C.T.U CLAIM EQUAL PAY FOR THE SEXES

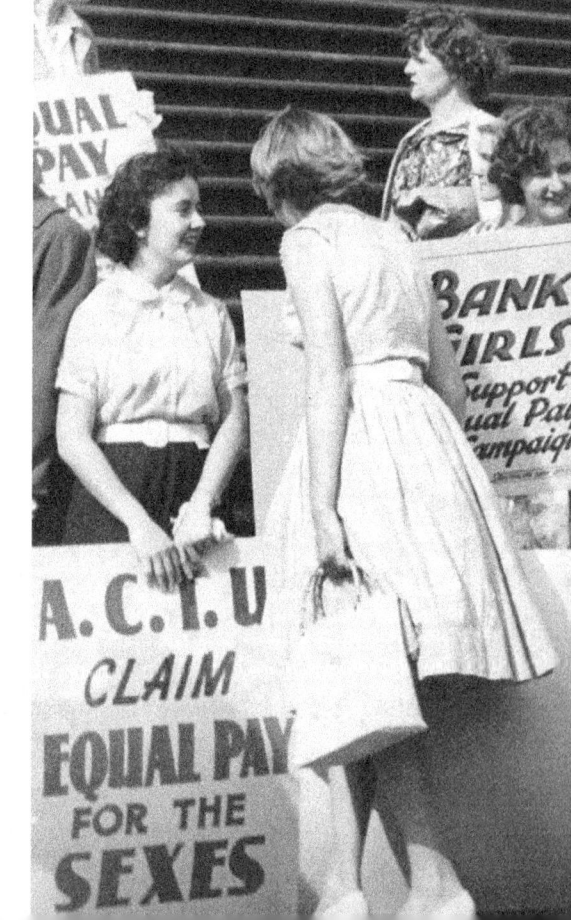

DEMAND
GOVERNMENTS
GRANT
EQUAL PAY
JUSTICE
TO WOMEN
DEMANDS
EQUAL PAY

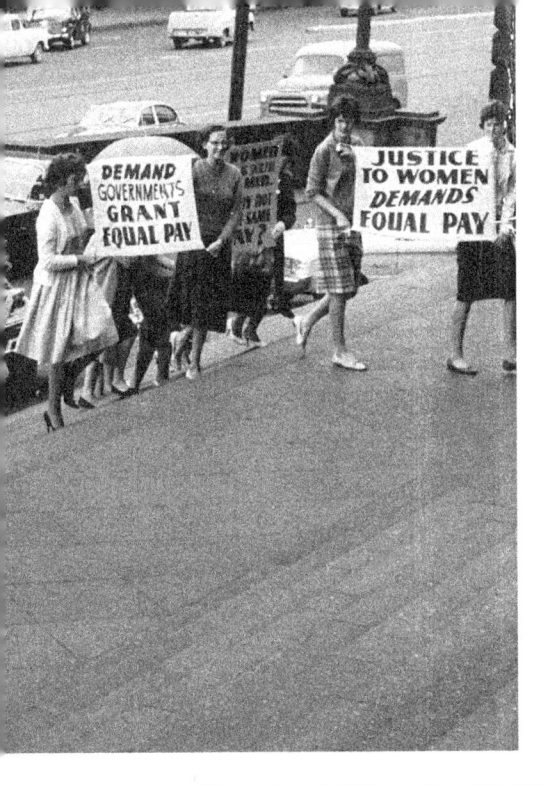

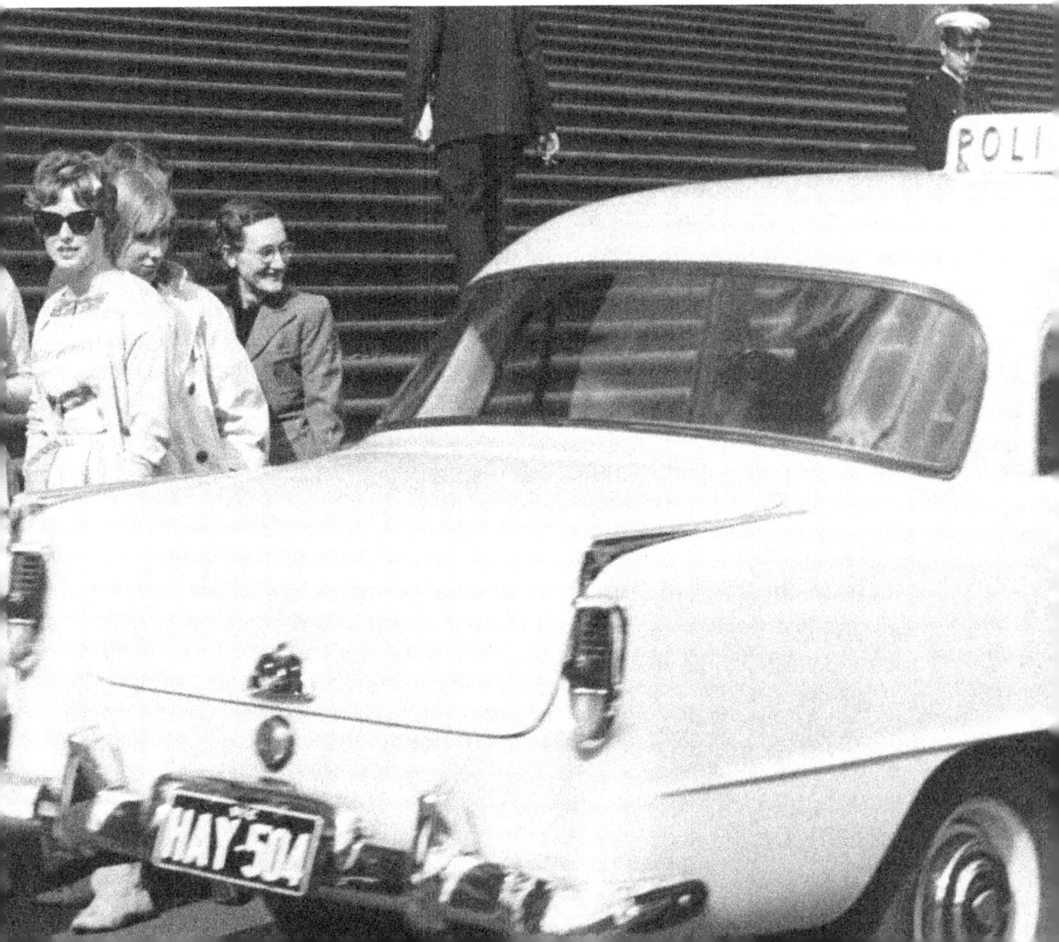
HAY-504

on struggles. In 1969, it published a prize-winning short story about a woman who enters an all-male workplace. The boss wants to start bringing in women on lower pay to replace the men. The heroine, who insists on equal pay, thwarts his plans.[19] There were quite a few small demonstrations on this and other issues. On IWD 1952, for example, the Newcastle group organised a 60-strong march to raise complaints about unemployment, housing, education, hospitals and food prices; a few days later, they travelled to Sydney to lobby state parliament. In 1964, 100 people attended an equal pay conference in Canberra.

The organisation was largely working class and extremely class-conscious. In 1963, *Our Women* reported favourably that men at Commonwealth Industrial Gases had struck for a fortnight against plans to employ females at pay lower than the male rate. Female canteen workers joined the strike. Both the canteen staff and the UAW saw the boss, rather than male workers, as their enemy.

The UAW helped to organise the union women's committees and worked to support strikes. It also devoted a lot of energy to home and community issues, although without the fire of the New Housewives. Members with children were usually active in the school Mothers' Club, working for a new library or a safe set of fire stairs or for better child care. Fourteen Melbourne members picketed the Gas and Fuel Corporation in 1962 in protest against price rises.

The peace movement, a huge issue for the communists, was also important for the UAW, which organised 'Peace Walks' in the face of government repression. In Perth, they were arrested and fined for 'parading with placards'. The 'placards' were actually aprons and scarves emblazoned with peace slogans. After a successful Supreme Court appeal against the convictions, other branches were emboldened to stage similar actions. These continued through the 1960s, and there was continuing repression. A short story published in *Our Women* in 1964 gives some impression of what the participants were up against, both in the streets and at home:

> What would the family say? They would be horrified when they knew she had taken part in a 'Ban the Bomb' demonstration. She didn't really mind going to court herself, she was quite happy to stand up for what they had done. None of them considered they had broken the law. They had simply printed, large on their wearing apparel, words calling for a peaceful world, and walked around the city footpaths.

The woman's husband hears about the event from the newspaper and is upset. Why didn't she tell him?

'You ought to know why I didn't tell you,' Helen was almost in tears. 'You always criticise everything I do. Some silly women's ideas you'd say. As if women can't think for themselves. I suppose we should stay in the kitchen like our mothers and grandmothers, and go on rearing gun-fodder.'[20]

Finally, the UAW kept alive the tradition of IWD. We sometimes read that IWD began with the Women's Liberation Movement, while more informed writers realise that it began as part of the working-class struggle and the socialist movement early in the 20th century. Hardly anyone recalls the UAW's IWD luncheons with political speakers. While the focus was normally on standard women's rights issues, other concerns were included. In 1965, the Newcastle group invited Aboriginal poet Oodgeroo Noonuccal (then known as Kath Walker) to address them.

The Newcastle group also provoked some controversy by appointing a male IWD organiser in the early 1960s. Barbara Curthoys recalls:

There was opposition from some women in other cities, but Merv Copley was a good organiser and he succeeded in having IWD recognised and supported by male trade union leaders.[21]

The UAW declined in the 1960s and 1970s. The first major setback came with the Sino–Soviet conflict; a minority of pro-China communists broke away from both the party and the UAW, and the factional strife drove others away. A second split in 1971 between Soviet-liners and those increasingly critical of Moscow was a further blow. *Our Women* ceased publication around this time.

However, the most important factor was a changing social climate. A new era of industrial militancy and political radicalisation began around 1967. Government hostel workers demonstrated for equal pay, as did psychiatric nurses. Barmaids took action around the issue and won. Teachers in NSW won equal pay, to be phased in from 1967. By 1969, the Arbitration Commission's refusal to grant equal pay to more than a token number of employees provoked a small group of Melbourne women to chain themselves to public buildings. Their Action Committee proved to be a forerunner of the Women's Liberation Movement. The communists, who had settled into a relatively conservative style of work, were suddenly outflanked by new forces on the left. There was a political gap between the women's liberationists and the UAW, as one of the latter told me:

REBEL WOMEN

"Women March For Peace" demonstration in Newcastle. These marches were a feature of International Women's Day celebrations on March 8 in Sydney as well. 1963

IWD rallies in Newcastle: (from top) 1948, 1963 and 1964

When Women's Lib started, some of the older women were a bit shocked by some of the things that went on in Women's Lib, and they wouldn't have a bar of that. The younger women felt this, and they sort of felt that the UAW was old hat. They didn't want to have a bar of it or anything to do with it.[22]

The more militant UAW members did find their way into Women's Liberation. Others, like Betty Olle, saw the Women's Electoral Lobby as the 'seventies success story'[23] and the best place to work. Either way, new forces were pushing aside the old.

Equal pay protest by female council workers, Melbourne Town Hall, 20 February 1969.

5
Militant action among white-collar workers
The struggle for equal pay in the insurance industry 1973-75

DIANE FIELDES

It is over 40 years since Australia's first ever national strike by clerical workers. The issue that drove insurance workers, male and female, to this action was equal pay. The fight for it showed how a common *class* interest could begin to bridge sexist divisions among workers. In the course of the campaign, workers of both genders attended meetings in their thousands, banned overtime, marched in the streets and demonstrated outside insurance companies. The driving force was the union rank and file. The union, whose members had never struck before, gained hundreds of new members, and the campaign created a new attitude to women workers.

The Australian Insurance Staffs' Federation (AISF) was founded in 1920 as part of the growth in white-collar unionism following World War I. A special meeting of female members in 1927 affirmed the principle of equal pay for both genders, and the Federal Executive then adopted it as AISF policy. None of this made much impact on the insurance companies, however; they continued to benefit from low pay for women workers.

Despite its early support for the principle of equal pay, the AISF's position was by no means unambiguous. The contradictory attitudes displayed did not represent a simple division along gender lines. In the union's first decade, some male workers supported the displacement of male labour by cheaper female workers.[1] This arose, not from any lack of gender loyalty by the men, but from their lack of class-consciousness. Their loyalty to their employers was such that they wished to ensure profitability even at the cost of jobs for their own gender. On the other hand, the 1939 Federal Council meeting of the AISF expressed concern about a repeat of the post-World War I experience, where women employed in wartime stayed on into the peace. The union warned against the 'flooding' of offices with women.[2]

Not until the 1960s did the equal pay issue again gather momentum. The AISF's journal, *Premium*, shows a gradual acceleration from 1966 in the number and length of articles dealing with equal pay. Conference motions in 1967, 1969 and 1971 also reflected greater pressure for equal pay.

In 1969, the ACTU won a case in the Arbitration Commission, resulting in the first national decision granting a form of equal pay to women.[3] Where women did 'equal work' with men, they would receive equal remuneration. However, the Commission excluded cases 'where the work in question is essentially or usually performed by females but is work upon which male employees may also be employed'.[4] By the time the ACTU returned to the Commission with further demands in 1972, only 18 percent of women workers had benefited from the 1969 decision.

The combination of increasing numbers of women in the workforce and the rise of the Women's Liberation Movement in Australia at the end of the 1960s directed unions' attention to questions concerning women workers. Changes in the employment needs of Australian capitalism had seen growing numbers of females, especially married women, drawn into the paid workforce. By the early 1970s, almost one-third of Australia's workers were female. Alongside this went changes in the nature of white-collar work. The process of proletarianisation is vital to understanding the equal pay campaign. In insurance, prior to the 1970s, new male entrants had expected well-defined career prospects. Increasingly, however, the insurance industry no longer offered a 'career' for the majority of its workers. Instead, part-time and 'dead-end' lower tier jobs, particularly for women, increased. These factors created a workforce that was increasingly female, very young, relatively poorly paid and with a very high labour turnover. A further outcome was the 'feeling that they are no longer treated with appreciation and respect by employers' – which could lead not only to unionisation, but also to greater militancy.[5]

AISF officials interviewed in Gerard Griffin's study of the union especially favoured two factors to explain the changed industrial behaviour of white-collar workers. One was youth; the other was working-class background. As white-collar work expanded, the bulk of those entering no longer came from white-collar family backgrounds. Griffin's survey of insurance union members (conducted in 1979) found a substantial number of respondents from 'working class backgrounds'. The largest single group (36 percent) described their father's occupation as 'manual'. Forty-one percent had at least one parent who was a trade union member.[6]

Another feature influencing the AISF in its fight to win equal pay was the general political and industrial situation. Phil Reilly, federal president of the AISF in this period, remarked:

I'm inclined to think that the activity of our union was part of a reflection of the change in society. Don't forget, in the 1960s and 1970s there was a great upsurge of activity in society. The Vietnam War was a catalyst to all sorts of shedding of old shackles, particularly among the young people.[7]

The rise of the Women's Liberation Movement at the end of the 1960s had a direct effect on the struggle for equal pay. With increasing numbers of women in the workplace, wage inequality was an obvious target for the movement's attention. Activists joined the picket lines of striking Sportsgirl machinists and supported Melbourne tram conductresses trying to get jobs as drivers. The movement's orientation to women as workers affected the unions; for example, the Victorian Branch of the Clothing and Allied Trades Union participated in some Women's Liberation committees in the early 1970s.

Added to this was the ability of the union movement to win campaigns. The late 1960s and early 1970s saw the union movement taking up questions of wages more vigorously than in the past. This led not just to a rising level of industrial action, but also to a series of significant victories. In 1969, a major, semi-spontaneous strike wave had defeated the government's and Arbitration Commission's attempt to fine unions (and jail union officials) for taking industrial action. The AISF itself had taken its first overt industrial action in 1970 over a wage claim. A successful campaign for a pay rise in 1972–1973, involving overtime bans and stopwork meetings, followed. Victories such as this laid the basis for greater union confidence to go on the offensive over wages, including equal pay for women. Thus, the equal pay fight was part of a more general working class radicalisation, reflected also in union action for Aboriginal and Torres Strait Islander rights; against a touring South African rugby team; for gay and lesbian rights; and against destruction of the environment.

A slow start to the campaign

In March 1970, the AISF produced a special equal pay edition of *Premium*, giving a chronology of the effect of the Arbitration Commission's 'equal pay for equal work' decision. After approaching the insurance employers' association, the Staffs' Reference Committee (SRC), in 1969, the AISF had been denied negotiations on equal pay. Following this, the AISF leaders hastened very slowly. Not until July 1972, more than three years after the Commission's first equal pay decision, could they announce: 'Federation acts on equal pay. Negotiations begin with SRC.' The claim for equal pay required the deletion of the 'female scale' of pay and the application of the 'male scale' to all workers.[8]

Meanwhile, grievances were accumulating in the offices. Women in the insurance industry aged 16 received 100 percent of the male rate of pay; at 21, they got 82 percent; at 34, women received 62 percent of the male rate. Wages in insurance were more unequal than in many other industries, because of increasing divergence between the genders with increases in seniority. Rather than simply having a junior and an adult rate, the wage scale in insurance was a particularly extended one. For men, there was the possibility of a wage increase for each of the first 14 years of service. For women in the industry, such increases ceased after seven years. At the top of the scale, a woman insurance worker was receiving only 7.63 percentage points better than the 54 percent of the male rate awarded to women workers by the Arbitration Commission in 1919. Perhaps the inequities rankled more in insurance, where women made up half the workforce, compared to 33 percent of the total Australian workforce at the time.

The insulting attitudes that accompanied unequal pay provided another source of agitation. During World War II, insurance employers had used the demeaning practice of issuing 'incompetency certificates' to employees who, for any reason, were not able to perform at a 'desired level'. This allowed for wages even lower than the amount specified in the award to be paid to selected employees. This selection process strongly 'favoured' women. By the 1960s, it was commonplace for senior women to train young men who were then promoted to pay scales above them. The *maximum* rate for a woman was less than that for a 21-year-old man.

Kevin Davern, an official of the South Australian and Victorian branches of the AISF during the equal pay campaign, remembered that:

> it would constantly be used that women couldn't be seen as equal because typewriters at the time were very heavy...[and what if] somebody had asked me to move their typewriter?... Everybody was 'girls' in the minds of the management.[9]

Women workers sometimes hid the fact that they had children, in order to secure employment in an industry where the expectation was that such responsibilities and full-time employment were incompatible. No wonder bitterness was growing.

Dissatisfied with the narrowness of the 1969 'equal pay for equal work' decision, the unions approached the Arbitration Commission again. In December 1972, the Commission agreed to widen its interpretation of equal pay to 'equal pay for work of equal value'. Pay increases under this decision were to be phased in by the middle of 1975. The AISF officials lodged a claim for equal pay on these terms in March 1973. Again, their demand was to delete the 'female scale' from the award and put all workers onto the 'male scale'. The employers countered this with the claim that any adjustment to women's wages would have to be contingent upon evaluation and reclassification of *all* positions in the industry.

After four years of non-cooperation from the employers, the AISF leadership at last moved to consider action on equal pay. The final straw was the SRC's consultants' report, which would have placed women in the lowest classifications, with pay not very much higher than their existing (unequal) rates. The employers saw these arrangements as discharging in full their obligations to provide equal pay. The union refused to accept the plan.

There were important differences: between the full-time officials of the union and the rank and file membership, and between female and male members. The AISF leaders' eyes were firmly fixed on negotiations, which would lead to an arbitrated settlement. They only sought membership action to push the negotiations in a favourable direction or to influence the Arbitration Commission. From this point of view, members' enthusiasm could even appear as a problem. General Secretary Ken McLeod complained of 'a view amongst some sections of the membership that equal pay means the removal of all female rates of pay from the award', leading to 'expectations which might well be impossible to realise'.[10]

Generally, however, the officials thought that members were apathetic or even hostile to the campaign. When interviewed in 1978, McLeod recalled mid-1973 as a time when it was 'hard to sell the members' on the issue; in his report to Federal Executive after the meetings, he had spoken of 'wide spread and deep-seated opposition to equal pay both from males and females.'[11] Similarly, an academic study of the AISF attributes the success of the equal pay campaign to 'the determination and influence of the leadership and the poor strategy and tactics of the employers.'[12]

Yet, other evidence from the union's records suggests a more complex picture. While there may have been hostility, there was also enthusiasm. A one-sided concern with antagonism to equal pay could mean that the union leadership failed to mobilise those who did want to fight. By mid-1973, the subject was likely to come up even at small, local meetings. After one such event, Victorian Branch Secretary Alleyn Best reported:

Marchers at IWD Sydney 1975 call for equal rights for women.

> Sandra [Fenn] and the members there are extremely union minded...
> They still regard the negotiations with suspicion and wonder what will
> happen with equal pay. They are very keen to be involved in the equal
> pay campaign... It appears, too, that they are getting good support on this
> from the men.[13]

But there is little evidence of the union addressing the concerns of members like these.

The contradiction between the officials and the ranks was sharpened by a core of activists who based themselves on membership dissatisfaction. The thorn in the side of the AISF officials was a small group of socialists producing a fortnightly leaflet, *Clerk and Dagger*. This news-sheet often ran articles criticising leaders of the various clerical unions; by mid-1973, it had begun to turn its attention more specifically to equal pay in insurance. The *Clerk and Dagger* group spawned an offshoot called Militant Insurance Clerks (MIC), whose newsletter was *Miccy Finn*. To suggestions of membership apathy, MIC replied:

> So far the union has paid little more than lip service towards equal pay...
> At the moment, the bureaucrats are saying that they're doing everything
> possible because women don't want equal pay! They think that women
> are not prepared to act because there has been no rash of wildcat strikes
> over the issue. The truth is that they have misinterpreted the good
> faith of women who believe that they can expect the union to lead any
> necessary campaign.[14]

MIC activists sought to relate to those who were enthusiastic about equal pay, in order to push the campaign forward. In three weeks, they were able to gather the signatures of 460 insurance workers in Melbourne (over 10 percent of the membership) and 50 supporters on a petition demanding an industrial campaign to win equal pay. The AISF leadership's only response was a suggestion that they might like to get some of the non-members who signed the petition to join the union. In fact, the petitioning process had already resulted in a number of people joining.[15]

There were also divisions between male and female members. Of course, there is a considerable temptation to identify the supporters of equal pay as female and its detractors as male. Griffin attributes apathy over the issue to the fact that it 'would not have meant a cent more in the pockets of the male members'.[16] So let's consider who in the membership supported equal pay. There is evidence of young women like Marie O'Donnell and Sandra Fenn at RACV, and others who had become radicalised, supporting equal pay:

> There was a lot of young women who may not have had a principled position on it but were becoming radicalized, and…they didn't have the same disciplines as the earlier generation had, and they were prepared to go to marches – they enjoyed it, you know![17]

But alongside them were young men like Ralph Clark in South Australia:

> [at] a meeting at Adelaide Town Hall… I recall myself and the president being booed by the middle-aged males as we went to the podium… I recall [Ralph Clark] …he's a large fellow, and he was a very young man at the time. We were under absolute stress at the time, and he walked from the back of the hall…and he said something that wouldn't be acceptable today but at the time the women, particularly young women, cheered him. He said to these men, 'All you know about the values of women is what you have tried to learn in the back seat of an FJ Holden.' And it did something to, I guess, polarize the total meeting.[18]

Phil Griffiths, a 20-year-old insurance clerk at the time, recalled that 'huge numbers of women were drawn into the union because it was fighting for equal pay' but acknowledged 'a moderate majority of men' at the rallies and mass meetings.[19]

While some men, especially older ones, were extremely hostile, there was also resistance to equal pay from some women. Again, there seems to have been a generational element:

> It was my experience in the office that there were more than a few women…whose attitude was 'Well, of course it's reasonable, we're going to go off and have babies'… It's easy to ridicule it now, but these were quite seriously held attitudes.[20]

> Initially [there was] quite a lot of resistance from the men in particular, and I suppose you could relate that very much to age… Generally speaking, the older the member, the more…definite they were that this [equal pay] was not a good thing… Women of course…were very much in favour of the notion but there were always a number of women in each

office who would say that this wasn't going to come to any good...that it wasn't right and that it was going to alter the relationship between men and women in general, in the family, in relationships, and so on, and all those things about, 'Well, men won't be opening doors for us any more and...taking us out to dinner'. That would always come up and again generally you'd be looking at...the older women in the industry... But they were the few.[21]

Because of the importance of seniority-based promotion in the insurance industry, the question of age could intersect with class. Those, overwhelmingly men, who had reached the senior managerial rungs of the promotions ladder were separated from the lower level clerical workers by class position rather than merely by age.

The view that gender determined attitudes could lead to some confusion. Jan Martin, female personnel manager at National Mutual, fought consistently against equal pay, often appearing for the employers in tribunal hearings. One AISF member recalled:

I was amused when I went down to this demonstration [at the Arbitration Commission] someone was holding a banner saying 'Is Jan Martin a woman?'[22]

Women-only?

The first meetings specifically about equal pay (on 25 September 1973) were generally small, but this can't be explained in terms of membership apathy or male hostility. Rather, we have to look at the basis on which they were held. The union leadership advertised them as 'women only'. They were not stopwork meetings but lunchtime ones, further limiting the number who could attend. Finally, they were not general meetings but meetings of 'representatives of AISF's female membership', comprising approximately 10 to 15 percent of members.

This initial round of meetings did provide evidence of some 'deep-seated opposition' - not to equal pay, but to the way the campaign was being conducted. The MIC bulletin said that the 'invitation only' form of the meeting had 'already alienated sections of the male and female membership', while *Clerk and Dagger* reported that female members in some offices had crossed out the 'women only' on official notices. Geelong members wrote to the Victorian Branch Committee of Management, criticising the exclusion of men and the fact that it was not a stopwork meeting.

It is hardly surprising that activists who opposed the leadership reported such incidents. But the most telling evidence comes from the official minutes of the Melbourne meeting. The Federal Executive's resolution had been carried unamended by meetings in Sydney, Brisbane and Adelaide. However, at the best-attended of all the meetings, Sandra Fenn and Marie O'Donnell from RACV Insurance in Melbourne moved a hostile amendment. They objected to the meeting being described as 'this meeting of representatives of AISF's female membership' and deleted the reference to 'female'. They added a call for the executive to prepare plans for industrial action and present them to the membership. Finally, they rejected the proposal for 'similar meetings to this' to be held throughout the campaign, calling instead for 'stop-work meetings of the membership'. Their amendment was carried.[23]

In planning the 1973 equal pay campaign, the leadership again argued that 'men should be encouraged to view the introduction of equal pay as a "union issue" rather than exclusively as a "women's issue"', and 'any campaign on equal pay should seek to involve the whole membership'. Yet, in practice, the campaign began with a women-only meeting of office representatives, followed a month later by mass meetings of women. Only after that, at the end of October 1973, were the first mass meetings of all members to be called. Some of this was argued for on the positive basis of encouraging women to lead and develop campaign activity. The negative side of launching the campaign in this way was that it undercut the idea that equal pay concerned the entire membership.[24] To the extent that the AISF leadership accepted the assumption that the male members would not be interested in equal pay (an assumption which apparently did not apply to male union leaders, whose reports took up most of the limited meeting time),[25] they launched the equal pay campaign on a weaker and more divided footing than necessary. Interviewed almost two decades later, Ken McLeod unwittingly reinforced this point:

> When we started to get the guys involved in it and they could see, on the one hand, that their jobs weren't threatened and, on the other hand the women could see they weren't going to be pushed out of the industry...it started to take off.[26]

Arguments about the importance of equal pay as an issue for all union members, regardless of gender, continued to be aired. In July 1973, *Premium* published an article, 'Equal pay – Equal to what? One member's view' by Phil Griffiths, a clerk at Royal-Globe Life Insurance and a *Clerk and Dagger* activist. Griffiths argued that, far from being irrelevant to male workers, the lack of equal pay was a positive *disadvantage* to them:

> The main reason that men have won a substantial career scale and better wages is that they have always organised themselves more effectively to resist low wages... Because the union has not been seen to defend the wages of women...it has not been able to organise women into the union to fight for the interests of all insurance staff... It is a vicious circle and one that has harmed the interests of all insurance workers... [The union] must work to convince the male membership that their future lies in fighting with women for their mutual individual interests.[27]

Griffiths pointed out that, while male and female workers were disadvantaged by unequal pay, their employers gained financially and ideologically:

> low wages paid to women continue to give employers a cheap more economical choice when hiring staff...[and] by dividing men from women workers [through fear of women taking their jobs] employers strengthened their industrial position and enlisted the support of men to keep the wages of women as low as possible, and thus continued to serve their major interest – profit – at the expense of their employees.[28]

The campaign takes off

Word of how employers were using reclassification as a way to avoid equal pay had spread through the clerical workforce by late 1973. An unnamed Melbourne institution was said to have reclassified all its male workers as 'administrative assistants' and its females as 'clerks'. 'Equal pay' then meant a small immediate pay rise for women but a shortened career scale. *Nation Review* claimed that insurance companies were already pooling women in clerical departments, with a view to classifying the lowest paid jobs as female. Cases such as those of 'typists' who spent three days a week on clerical work (supposed to be higher paid than typing) were becoming a talking point.

When the SRC made its equal pay offer in October 1973, such fears about reclassification proved justified. The offer reduced the female scale for adults from seven steps to four, effectively putting a lower ceiling on women's wages. It also required the union's agreement to an overall classification scheme *before* any wage increases were paid. The union leaders called a series of mass meetings and asked how long it would be before companies tried to cut men's wages in the same way. They quoted the SRC's own words:

> The inevitable introduction of equal pay is the reason why classification is highly desirable for all lower level jobs. Classification will allow a reduction in the cost of lower level jobs carried out by older males.[29]

The following day, 2,000–3,000 insurance workers (at a time when their Victorian branch had around 5,000 members) made their anger known at a demonstration outside the National Mutual building in Melbourne, while the SRC and the AISF leadership met inside it. The demonstrators voted to stay out for the rest of the afternoon and to have another stopwork a week later. Griffiths recalled:

> The next day [9 November 1973] proved everyone's hesitations wrong... I don't think [the union officials] even had a public address system there, or if they did it was of the megaphone variety. I think they expected 50 people, and there were...3,000... It was just jam-packed...and the sense of anger was tremendous... I remember going back into the office, completely fired up, racing around the office saying 'That's it! We're on strike. Come on, let's get going.'... Some came out, we all had these furious debates and the management came out and said, 'Look...if you're going to go on strike, go on strike, but you're not allowed to disrupt the office'... The mood was just tumultuous.[30]

The employers still held out for reclassification of the whole industry as a precondition for equal pay. Their next offer, on 26 November, was accompanied by a propaganda offensive. Companies addressed their workers directly as individuals, in an attempt to undermine the collective struggle. Commercial Union's 'Memorandum to all staff' began with special pleading about the insurance industry's inability to meet the Arbitration Commission's equal pay deadline of 30 June 1975, because of the complications of a seniority-based pay scale. It went on to argue for job evaluation as part of equal pay: the Commission's 1972 decision 'means that male rates must be determined in the same way [i.e., work value comparisons] and necessitates an evaluation of all jobs'.[31]

Such epistles probably did little to placate insurance workers once they saw what had been offered. The SRC's proposal barely narrowed the gap between women's and men's wages: the lowest paid women workers were offered an extra $1.04 a week. No indication was given as to how or when the remaining gap would be closed. But there was a further sting: the extra money was still tied to reclassification. The ceiling placed on salary increases for women under this 'equal pay' offer could be used to hold down male salaries as well in future.

This deadlock between employer intransigence and the growing anger of the members prompted the calling of the union's (and the Australian clerical industry's) first national strike on 14 December. Less than two months previously, the Federal Executive had worried about 'widespread and deep-seated opposition' among members. Now, it called on them to engage in unprecedented militancy over equal pay.[32]

It is undoubtedly true that members' outlook had changed. The actions they themselves had engaged in during the second half of 1973 (and the concessions they had won) showed equal pay *was* achievable if they kept the pressure on – and also that *only* such actions were likely to force further improvements. Recognition of this shift obviously encouraged the leadership to propose industrial action in November–December 1973. Still, they had not moved far from their original view of the campaign as one centred, in the final analysis, on negotiations and arbitration. The Federal Executive still proposed a national strike in hopes that the:

> threat of such a stoppage...[would place] the SRC and Arbitration Commission under pressure to settle the dispute in the time between December 7th and December 14th.[33]

Members were enthusiastic. Again, Melbourne members were the most active: 2,000–3,000 members voted to strike and then marched once again to the National Mutual plaza. Despite reported comments by the chair of the SRC, Mr J. L. Greig, that management 'had made a sincere and genuine offer to help relieve the situation', AISF members remained unconvinced.[34]

In the week before the strike, the employers tried to play on the fears of workers who had never struck before. The union responded:

> All members must consider themselves bound by this decision... Striking is the only responsible action to be taken in support of gaining justice... If you have never been on strike before, then here are a few hints: –

8/11/72 No 2.

A newsletter for clerical employees. We print the news and raise hell.

WALTONS EMPLOYEES LEFT IN THE LURCH

Waltons, the big Bourke Street retailer, recently started its insurance subsidiary in Melbourne. All was fine until the women working behind the counter, selling the insurance and collecting premiums found they were being paid *below the award!* As members of the Australian Insurance Staffs Federation, they contacted their local branch (Victoria) to complain. Waltons said that as they work in a shop, they were being paid shop assistant wages, $5 to $10 a week *less.* Apparently, the fact that the women are part of the Insurance industry, subject to the Insurance industry award to which Waltons is a signatory, did not seem to matter.

So what was the union's attitude to all this? Despite the fact that the Waltons staff is very heavily unionised, the union is *completely unwilling* to protect the wages of these members. Six months since the women approached the union, it is still considering the *"legal"* position.

Rank and file insurance workers group publication Clerk and Dagger

Be proud of the action you are taking... Disregard arguments against striking, particularly people who say there are 'reasonable' arguments against striking. After all, are the employers being 'reasonable'?[35]

Meanwhile, the AISF was also trying to reach a settlement in the Arbitration Commission. After hearings before Justice Elizabeth Evatt on Tuesday 11 and Thursday 13 December, the Federal Executive met the day before the strike. On a motion from delegate Steve Crabb, they decided to call it off – as long as the

General Secretary was satisfied with the day's final offer – despite the executive's preceding decision to refer any offer back to mass meetings. The executive cancelled the strike at the eleventh hour.

The wage rate handed down by the Arbitration Commission was identical to the SRC's last offer, up to step 4. However, it lifted the ceiling on women's wages up to the seventh year of adult service, although it did nothing about parity with the male 14-year scale. While it was not equal pay, it did also remove the threat of downward classification contained in the previous offer.

We cannot know whether the members themselves would have accepted this offer, so little different from that which had prompted them to vote for strike action. *Clerk and Dagger* concluded that the AISF officials never intended a strike, but had simply used the threat as a bargaining device. Allowing members to vote on the offer could have upset this strategy. In fact, the next issue of *Premium* stated:

> at that stage a strike could not have had any bearing on the result. Members had already displayed their solidarity, and this was of great help in the negotiations.[36]

The tone of the union leadership's explanation for cancelling the strike was defensive:

> In negotiations where an offer is made which requires acceptance, the Federation makes every effort to consult the membership. However, *the agreement was not an offer, it was a dispute settlement formula*, put forward by Justice Evatt.

Yet the question raised in *Clerk and Dagger* remained: if the apparently immovable SRC could be shifted away from the demand for reclassification by the mere *threat* of a strike, what might more serious industrial action have won?[37]

The proposition was not tested. It took another two years before formal equal pay for insurance workers was granted, but the union took no strike action in that time. The SRC continued, in a series of meetings with the union, to advance its claims for a classification scheme to cover the entire industry. In July 1974, forgoing negotiation, they simply asked the union to accept the classification scheme that the employers had devised. The AISF refused. September 1974 saw the union's membership begin another round of office reps' meetings. This sign that industrial action might revive, along with an overall industrial climate where equal pay was being granted across the workforce, produced an interim decision from the Commission on 1 November 1974 awarding a 5 percent increase to adult women.

A gap still remained between female and male wages. The insurance companies, now organised as the Insurance Employers' Industrial Association (IEIA), made a further offer towards equal pay on 5 September 1975. The union rejected it and decided to seek arbitration on the long-running dispute. As Griffin points out, both the 1974 and 1975 movements towards equal pay in insurance took place at Arbitration Commission direction, rather than in direct response to the sort of industrial pressure that had been built up in 1973. The motivating force was much more the general industrial and political climate, in which inequality was seen as increasingly intolerable. But the AISF members did provide one last push. The union's conference adopted a proposal to declare 16 October 1975 'National Insurance Industry Equal Pay Day', with an Australia-wide stopwork from 2 pm to 3 pm and demonstrations. In Melbourne, 1,000 members marched from their offices to reach the Arbitration Commission at 2 pm.

On 15 November 1975, Commissioner Paine granted equal pay up to the seventh year of adult service. The decision did still leave a loophole through which lower wages for women (and increasingly for junior men) could persist. The union leaders were aware of it, and it was to keep union organisers busy in the coming years. The pay scale still allowed for workers who performed routine duties more than 50 percent of the time to have their wages frozen at the seventh step.

Outcomes and conclusions

The effects of this campaign were not confined to the extra money women workers now received – fortnightly increases ranging from $6.88 to $79.31. Significant changes had also taken place in the nature of the AISF and in the attitude to women that existed inside it. There was a growing class-consciousness – an 'us and them' attitude towards the employers. The common struggle had begun to break down sexist divisions in the workforce.

The union grew. Writing in 1977, Russell Lansbury argued that, among the elements likely to contribute to the growth of white-collar unionism in the future, was the fact that:

> given a continuation of the current industrial environment in Australia in which the more assertive unions win higher rewards for their

members, white-collar employees are likely to become more militant. Indeed, it may be argued that white-collar workers will not improve their position while they maintain a belief in intelligent and mutually trusting cooperation as the foundation of their relations with employers.[38]

The growth of the AISF at the time of the equal pay campaign (and the wage campaign which preceded it in 1972) bears out Lansbury's argument. The union gained 1,693 new members in 1972 and 1,127 in 1973, after a small decrease in membership in 1971. To explain this growth (13.3 percent in 1972 and 7.8 percent in 1973), Griffin argues that 'evidence points to increased membership as a direct role of industrial action'.

This is certainly reinforced by the AISF General Secretary's report on the union's 1972 salary campaign, its only widespread industrial action prior to that on equal pay. He estimated that 7,500 members attended stopworks in December 1972 – a very high figure. Conversely, he pointed out that, where there was no campaign activity – as in the Western Australian branch – 'membership...is at its lowest level for the past decade and the morale of the membership probably at a similar level'. Phil Griffiths recalled that one feature of the 3,000-strong equal pay meeting in Melbourne on 5 December 1973 was the number of non-members present. He went back to his office after the vote to strike and 'started signing people up because there was going to be a strike'.[39]

A report to the Victorian branch's 1973 annual general meeting noted unprecedented growth, a 25 percent increase in collection of union dues and a 50 percent reduction in arrears. Where people were actively involved, and the union appeared to be fighting for their rights, commitment of all sorts increased. On the other hand, the reversal of the AISF's growth coincided with a period (21 December 1973 to August 1975) in which no industrial action whatsoever took place in the insurance industry. In 1974, membership *declined* by 332, although the experience of the previous two years might have suggested a growth of over 1,000.[40]

The AISF began to act much more like a trade union than a professional association. Some writers attribute the changes to the role of specific figures in the leadership. Others who were union officials at the time, such as Kevin Davern, also give some weight to this factor:

There was a period, up until the mid-60s, when the union was a bit of a club. The fellows controlled it, but also they did it on the basis that there had never been an industrial dispute... It was people coming back from the war like Phil Reilly [federal president], who were seen as mad lefties by the establishment, who changed that. Ken McLeod...had a powerful influence because he succeeded a guy who was federal secretary who was a Liberal.[41]

Much more important, however, was the self-activity of the union members, in what *Premium* called 'the most extensive and extended industrial action ever undertaken by the Federation.'[42] A narrow view of the union as one that 'just looked after the people who intended to be in insurance until they were 65' was not able to cope with the upsurge of anger over equal pay. The AISF was no longer a union where strike action was unthinkable.

The extent of the change can be gauged from the alternative industrial strategy proposed by the MIC in September 1973. The AISF leadership regarded this group as extremists whose proposals would derail the campaign. Yet, what was the MIC's proposal, less than three months before the members voted for a national strike? Insurance workers should withdraw their labour from key areas in every company. 'This recognises that full strike action in insurance is probably not feasible at the moment.'[43]

Workers' attitudes to each other also changed. Their common class position, as workers fighting the boss, began to bridge the gender divide. References to action 'in which men and women joined as equal partners', or the gratification felt by the Victorian branch president on seeing 'both males and females demonstrating together outside the Arbitration Court', illustrate this. It was difficult for male workers to go on seeing women as second-class citizens when they were fighting alongside them (and losing pay) to win equality. Employer attempts to use reclassification both to avoid equal pay and to push down male wages merely underlined the common class interest.[44]

Gleghorn, in his commissioned history of the insurance union, wrote:

> the achievement of equal pay, the union-wide heat it generated and a new attitude it created to women workers, was a million miles from [the] sexist jokes and equality on male terms of the earlier years of the Federation.

In an attempt to get women more involved, a 1968 edition of *Premium* had portrayed a stereotypical female wandering into a union meeting by accident and finding it wasn't too bad after all. Young men were not encouraged to join the union in this fashion. Such patronising appeals to women *entirely* disappeared from *Premium* by 1972, as did sexist cartoons.

The AISF's official structures also showed some signs of change. In May 1968, the Victorian branch elected the first woman secretary of a white-collar union in Australia. Diana Sonenberg had worked as an organiser since 1966. However, the article which announced her election also informed the reader that *Mrs* Sonenberg lived in a flat in Elwood with her two children, that she cooked dinner at night and that she managed to do her job 'with the help of two baby-sitters, her parents – and a lot of organization.'[45] Five years later, when a similar article announced the appointment of *Ms* Marian Miller as Federal Organiser to work in the Victorian branch, no such personal details were thought necessary. However, the improvement was not uniform. At the end of 1973, Marian Miller could still point out that only 10 percent of office reps were women, despite 60 percent female employment in the industry.[46]

It is often thought that equal pay emerged from the (somewhat belated) wisdom of the Arbitration Commission in its 1969 and 1972 equal pay decisions, and even that 'the period of implementation [of the 1972 decision] was remarkably uncontentious.'[47] The AISF experience suggests otherwise: it was union action, not the justice of the case that won gains for insurance workers. Lower pay for women had been no less unjust in 1962 when the AISF leadership had approached the prime minister to do something about it. At the time, *Premium* had commented: 'it is hoped that some announcement may be made during the budget session of Parliament.'[48]

Casting off such illusions in favour of industrial action was an important precondition for winning real gains. Despite tribunal decisions, unionists still had to fight their employers to achieve equality. Lansbury argues that 'the failure of arbitration to provide adequate protection for white-collar employees' was a factor causing their unions to adopt more militant tactics.[49] That was certainly true in the insurance industry.

Kortex strikers danced on the picket line and sang songs about the need for solidarity and cutting out union officials' tongues.

6
Sweatshop rebels
The 1981 Kortex strike
SANDRA BLOODWORTH

How quickly people can change! The December 1981 Kortex strike illustrates how women's oppression and their exploitation as workers combine and interact. A struggle in the workplace can spill over into the home and family life, with remarkable consequences.

Before the dispute, most of the women had never been involved in any struggle; there were no elected shop stewards, and they had almost no contact with their union officials. The men (and they were virtually all men) who claimed to be shop stewards were nothing but company stooges.

The Kortex workers seemed to fit the stereotype of passive, submissive, easily exploited migrant women. Yet their 10-day strike, involving 300 women, brought enormous transformations. In the course of the dispute, they had to fight cops wielding batons and wearing guns; they faced arrest; company thugs bullied them; and their employers intimidated them.

How did a workforce with no trade union experience or history of militancy, with problems of communicating because of several different languages, get involved in such a strike in the first place? The answer does not lie in that particular factory, nor in any perception of their own oppression and exploitation by the strikers themselves. That perception was only to emerge in the course of the struggle.

To see how it began, we must look at what was happening in the working class as a whole. After several years of recession and industrial defeat, the workers' movement was fighting back, recording 3 to 4 million strike days annually between 1979 and 1981. The Storemen and Packers and Transport Workers' (TWU) Unions, along with other militant sections of the labour movement, had won pay rises of $25 and more, as well as a shorter working week. Their victories had created an atmosphere of confidence and combativeness among weaker unions. When you drove around the northern and western suburbs of Melbourne, you would frequently find pickets of workers on strike for higher wages.

One of the women at Kortex had a husband working at Rowntree's chocolate factory, where they had won a pay rise by industrial action. Others had husbands working at Ford in Broadmeadows, where there had recently been a long and bitter stoppage. A very small number belonged to the VTEB, a revolutionary Turkish communist group who had been involved in the Ford strike. The printing shop next door was on strike. There was an atmosphere in the area that you could win wage rises, if you were prepared to fight. All that was needed was a spark to ignite the pent-up anger and militancy.

Ironically, the employers did not provide this spark; the officials of the Textile Workers' Union did, by failing to show up one Friday for a meeting about a $25 pay claim. Furious, the women walked out, making plans to picket the factory on the following Monday.

On the Monday morning, by the time 300 of them had picketed their factory, marched to another Kortex factory nearby and brought all the workers there out on strike, they began to feel their collective strength. Now, they began to talk bitterly of their oppression and super-exploitation, the conditions they had endured for years. They drew up a log of demands.

They wanted an end to the compulsory 'bonus' system. The so-called 'bonus' system meant that, if you didn't get the extra amount of work done for the bonus, you were sacked. Even if you did finish it, you never knew just how much it was worth; it seemed to change at the bosses' whim. They wanted a canteen, so they had somewhere decent to have lunch and tea breaks and wouldn't have to smoke in the toilets. And, speaking of tea breaks, they wanted more of them. They only ever had one a day. They wanted the right to visit the toilet when they chose and for as long as they chose. The existing system was two visits a day, and those for only three minutes. Any longer brought the supervisors to drag them back to work. Perhaps the most galling of all was the compulsory donations they had to make for the bosses' birthdays. They wanted that stopped.

So, after one day, this was no longer simply a fight over pay. One woman told me 'no Australians work here because it's not a factory, it's a jail.' For the first time, they had begun to break down the walls of that jail. As a result of their own activity, they began to see the world, and their position in it, in a new light.

Tuesday morning was to be a test of their newfound strength. And now their lack of trade union traditions – the very thing that had held them back before –

could be a source of strength. Even quite militant workers can be demoralised when their trade union officials refuse to support them. But these women had no conception of the union officials doing anything for them. When the officials refused to bring out the scabs working inside (about 10 to 12), the women's response was to say: 'We'll strengthen the pickets – and no one will get in to work.' These strikers had broken out of the bondage of a lifetime. They were not ready to sit quietly and be defeated.

So they strengthened the pickets. Again, unlike more experienced unionists, they had no concern for what others would think of them; they were not concerned about how they would look in the press. And, unlike many picketers closely allied to union officials, they welcomed support from socialists. When members of VTEB and the IS went to the pickets, we were treated as if it was the most natural thing in the world for us to be there. One day later in the week, when one TV camera crew followed me around, obviously hoping to prove that the picket was being run by 'outsiders', the women gathered around me and began chanting 'no money – no work' until the camera crew gave up the chase.

The strikers did not hesitate to defend themselves against violence. When the cops attacked them with batons, they used their shoes to beat them back. When the union officials called them 'a pack of animals', they were so angry that they drove the officials into the factory yard, to hide behind the fence with the Kortex owners and managers.

After the pickets had stopped a couple of trucks from entering the factory gates, the excitement and exuberance that erupted was so infectious that those visiting the picket found themselves caught up in Turkish dancing and learning songs about cutting out union officials' tongues. Whenever anything exciting or dangerous happened, the women made a high-pitched, trilling noise which echoed around the factory walls.

The use of their own cultural ways to strengthen the pickets probably explained why at least 80–100 women arrived daily by 7:30 am, after finishing as late as 11:30 the night before. You always felt welcome on the picket, and that there was some point in being there. Even when there was no new development in the struggle, there were always singing, dancing and discussions.

The lively atmosphere was particularly important in this dispute. In most strikes, the employers and managers keep a low profile. In this one, they played a very prominent role in trying to demoralise the pickets, organising scabs and directing the police. They probably had as little sleep as the picketers themselves. It was clear that the women's high spirits annoyed the bosses immensely. It became just as clear that, if the picketers could get to speak to any of the women trying to enter the factory, they could usually talk them out of it. The bosses went to absurd lengths to prevent this.

On Tuesday, when the afternoon shift was about to start, the managers used men we called the 'goons' (paid $25 an hour) and the police to surround women approaching the factory to try to escort them into work, past the pickets. But

they were fighting a losing battle. There were incidents where a handful of women were being hassled into the factory surrounded by three or four cops, two or three bosses and their thugs. When strikers went over and managed to talk to these women, they managed to draw them away from the intimidating group of men to join the picket. Then the picketers would erupt into wild excitement.

To be on that picket was to understand what sisterhood really means. They didn't talk about it, but it was there, because the women had a shared experience of common oppression and because they understood each other from working together, day in, day out. The only reason any woman went to work during the strike was out of fear. If the picketers could talk to her, they could overcome that fear.

One event illustrates how well they understood how to undermine their opponents' confidence. A group was approaching the factory when some of the Turkish women called out to them in Turkish. There were some quiet smiles, and an air of amusement which we didn't understand (not speaking Turkish). The new arrivals approached the police lines at the factory gate and looked as if they were about to go in to work. Several of the Turkish women left the picket and went over to them. After a few words between the two groups, they all walked back to the picket. At first, we thought that it was simply the same event we had witnessed many times. But the excitement this time had a different quality. Bursting with curiosity, we asked what was going on. They explained that they knew the women were coming to the picket, but had called out and told them to do what they had done, so as to make it look as if more women had been won away from the bosses.

Hired company goons intimidate picketers

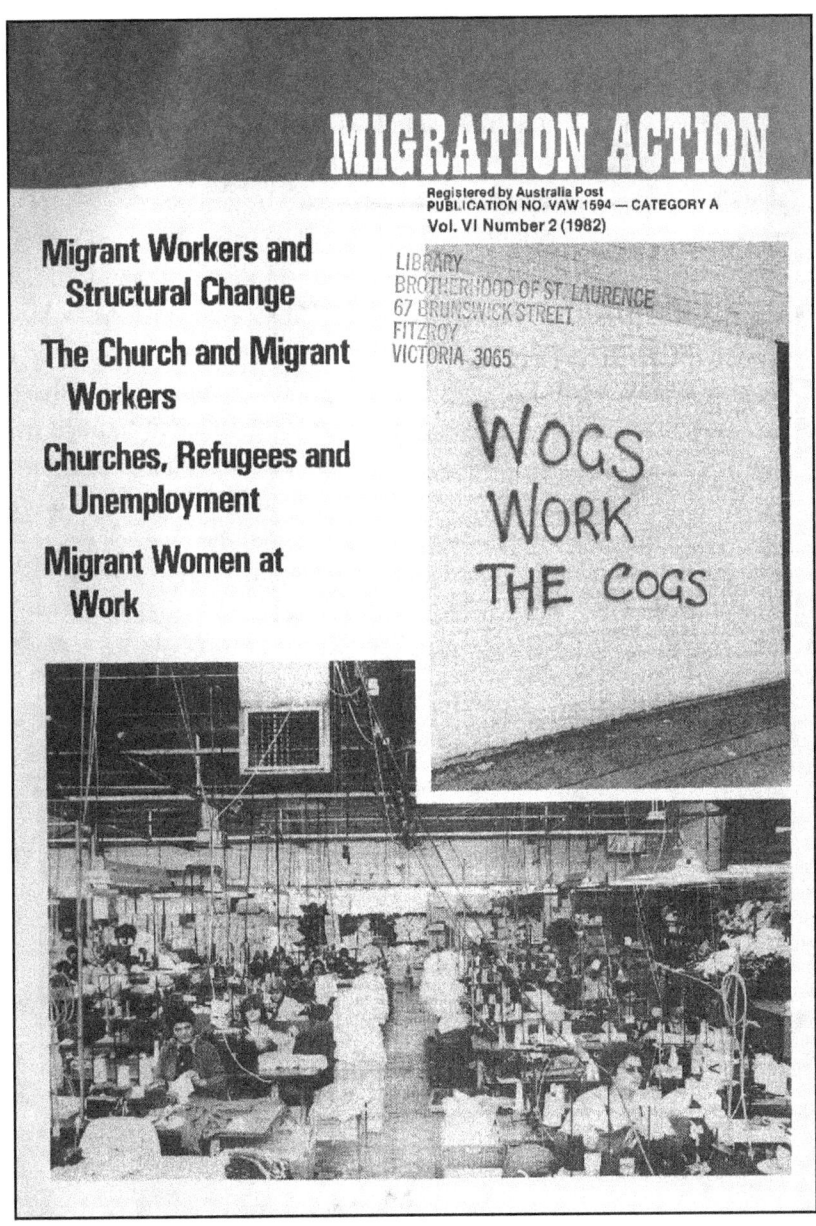

Migration Action, publication of the Ecumenical Migrant Centre, features a report on the Kortex strike.

The picketers had now established that they could effectively close down the factory, so the union officials called a mass meeting for the Wednesday morning. This seemed a potential stumbling block for the strikers: they had no knowledge of meeting procedures, they spoke many different languages (mainly Turkish, Greek, Arabic, Croatian and Italian), and few spoke English fluently. When busloads of women from other factories owned by Kortex began to arrive, it was clear that the bosses were determined to win – even by foul play.

They had leaflets in every language spoken in the factory, arguing for a return to work with the $13.50 the Arbitration Court had awarded to the whole industry. As far as anyone knew, the women in the bosses' bus weren't on strike anyway.

Unfortunately, the picketers had only been able to get leaflets translated into English, Turkish and Greek, but they had the edge on the employers. On that day, meeting procedure was not the main requirement. They needed courage, determination and the will to fight on whatever ground their opponents set.

The union officials made a show of only letting in union members at the door; but, somehow, the goons were all inside the hall when the meeting began. The officials were determined that the IS and VTEB members supporting the strike would not get in. But the striking women would have none of that. Some of them crowded onto the stage carrying placards saying 'no money – no work' and

Artwork from a 1982 edition of *Migration Action* depicts migrant women clothing machinists.

chanting slogans. Their response to provocation was no longer simply spontaneous; it was becoming more political. The trilling noise was more and more replaced by slogans which they had all learned in English. The women on the floor kicked up such a fuss that the officials had to throw out every one of the goons.

As a large proportion of the women were Turkish, Sultan spoke in English and Turkish. Sultan was a member of VTEB; her role, along with other members of VTEB in providing leadership throughout the strike, was important. They understood the importance of solidarity from outside; the need to keep all the strikers actively involved; the value of militancy; and politics. On this day, her speech was crucial in holding firm any women inclined to give in to the mounting pressure. Because of her role at the picket (arrested the first morning), she had a standing which any interpreters employed by the officials lacked. In fact, they were regarded with suspicion (as they are in many strikes involving migrants). And because of her own difficulty with English, she could use words and phrases which the women understood.

The strikers refused to vote any way other than by a division – and they won. The officials had no choice but to declare the strike official. They closed down the three Kortex factories in Melbourne. The television that night made great play of the fact that police were called in to stand between the two sides in the division. They were supposedly necessary to prevent the strikers from intimidating those who wanted to go back to work. Not a word about the intimidating tactics of the employers! This was an attempt to portray the strike as a fight between different groups of workers. Of course, picketers often do have to fight scabs who are people they have worked with. But, in this strike, the women knew that those who voted to go back did so out of fear. They wanted to win them over, not intimidate them.

A second mass meeting was called for Friday, to be held at Trades Hall. This time, the strikers had leaflets in Arabic as well. But the bosses were much better organised than the previous time: they had supplied a list of names which the union officials used to admit people to the meeting. Because the women on the pickets didn't know those from other factories, they couldn't be sure who was eligible and who wasn't. But it was clear that some of the company goons were being let in. As well, the factory owners and managers had megaphones and held placards saying 'We Want Work'. They were learning from the picketers how to hold a demonstration. However, try as they might, they couldn't get chants going with anywhere near the enthusiasm of the picketers.

The strikers didn't waste time being angry with the women alongside the bosses. They kept their anger for the bosses themselves, their goons, the police and the union officials. One of the employers went off trailing blood from his nose all down the corridors of Trades Hall. The air was stifling as hundreds of people crowded into the corridors. There were continual fights between the two sides, shouting, chanting and, occasionally, the high-pitched trilling. Amid all this, the picketers managed to steal one of the bosses' megaphones.

Inside the meeting, pandemonium broke loose when the officials announced a secret ballot (although the offer was the same as on Wednesday). The women for the strike were politically opposed to a secret ballot: they said that everyone should be willing to show where they stood in front of their work mates. But, just as importantly, they didn't trust the officials – a mistrust which was to prove well founded.

After a long argument, it became evident that the other side was going to vote, and the officials would use the votes to call off the strike. So those who wanted to continue the struggle decided to participate in many arguments going on in about five different languages. The scene was one of chaos, and this was to increase when they tried to lodge their votes in favour of staying out. The supervisors from the factory were guarding the ballot boxes. They were vetting the ballot papers, trying to tear up those for continuing the strike, and letting the other side vote more than once. Some of the women we knew from the pickets left the room and sat outside, refusing to even try to vote.

But the chaos frightened the employers, and they began trying to get the women back to the buses, declaring the whole thing a farce. They feared that the enthusiasm of the strikers would infect their own side, and the only way to be sure was to keep order and to keep both sides apart. During the ensuing bedlam, some of the VTEB men got into the meeting room. They began to attack some of the goons. But the women from the picket pushed them out of the way, yelling: 'Get out of the way, let *us* at them!' and using their shoes to good effect.

When the vote came out, it was 365 for staying out and 362 to go back – out of a meeting of no more than 500. The officials had set it up, so they had to accept the result. On talking to the strikers while driving back, we learnt that this victory had depended on the fighting spirit of the young women, some as young as 16. Some of them had fought their way in and voted up to 10 times. When we laughed, they simply replied: 'Some of the older women could not get ballot papers, so we had to vote for them.' They had learned lessons no amount of formal 'education' could teach them. Of course, the vote was a farce, but the strike had been saved – not by playing 'fair', but by sheer determination.

Over the weekend, the union officials and the bosses organised a meeting inside the factory for Monday morning. They sent out letters to the women's homes. That Monday morning, the officials were nowhere to be found, but it was soon obvious that a secret ballot was taking place. Being one of the few who spoke English, I rang the union office to find out where they were. I was told they were at the Kortex picket. So I rang the company, and said I was an organiser with the union. Were any officials or organisers there, please? 'Oh, yes,' came the reply, 'they're all here. Which one do you want?'

The employers had cars circling the neighbourhood picking up women and hustling them into the factory, with security guards and police keeping the pickets at a distance. The security guards were later called off the picket by their union, the Miscellaneous Workers. But the police provoked a violent confrontation and used the opportunity to arrest several people. One of the bosses gave an IS member a black eye.

The Kortex factory partly demolished in 2021. The working class history of places like Brunswick is rarely documented and is often lost to gentrification.

It became necessary to send in a delegation to find out what the offer was. That was the only time any of the women were afraid of the struggle. The thought of a small number having to go inside with police, bosses, thugs and union officials – without the support of the mass of strikers – almost made them lose their courage. Eventually, four or five volunteered to go with Sultan. They discovered that they were being offered an extra $11.50 at the end of March 1982, on top of the $13.50 granted by arbitration.

This was not a massive amount, and not as much as the militants wanted to hold out for, but it was still a victory. And that wasn't all. On the last day before the Christmas break, the women stopped work for a party – for the first time ever. The bosses were so nervous that they didn't say a word, and so the workers had won for themselves a half-holiday. Solidarity inside the factory was at an all-time high; some improvements were made in working conditions, and workers elected shop stewards.

It must be evident from the accounts of both the pickets and the mass meetings that the women's self-confidence grew enormously. Solidarity between the different migrant groups improved. But there was another important area of their lives which was greatly affected by the strike: relations between themselves and their families. There was never any suggestion that the struggle should be confined to the women themselves. This was not just in relation to their men, but also to socialists who offered help and support. Influenced by the revolutionary politics of VTEB members, they welcomed all the support they could get, while confidently running the strike themselves.

The men who came to the picket lines quite naturally fell in behind the women's leadership. They bought the coffee, minded children on the picket line and, where necessary, played an active role in the fighting. They helped translate leaflets and, at the mass meetings, it was mostly men and members of VTEB and the IS who handed them out. This freed the women to do more political work, such as preparing speeches, speaking to women who might be wavering or leading chants when the bosses' bus arrived.

Such work was more important than leafleting, but because those of us leafleting were more visible to the employers and union officials, they firmly believed that the strike would collapse if they could keep us away; that we were wholly responsible for this outbreak of what they considered completely unreasonable behaviour. This was a total misunderstanding. Outside supporters could provide backup, and sometimes advice; but, without the courage, creativity and will to fight of the Kortex workers, no amount of 'outside interference' could have made the strike happen.

Not only on the pickets did attitudes begin to change. In the homes, the men took over child care and house duties to free the women to attend the pickets for long hours. Here was an example of how women's issues and those of class exploitation are bound together; how a struggle can change attitudes and break down divisive stereotypes. As they fought to change their circumstances, the Kortex strikers also changed themselves and those around them.

DEDICATION DOESN'T PAY THE RENT!
WHITE LIES A CLAYTONS PAY RISE
SUPPORT the NURSES who CARE FOR YOU!
IRENE DIDN'T MAKE ME DO IT DAVID DID.

Dedication doesn't pay the rent!
The 1986 Victorian nurses' strike

LIZ ROSS

Nurses are often seen as the archetypal 'handmaidens' of men. If ever an experience demolished this image, it was the Victorian nurses' strike of 1986, in which a predominantly female workforce took on and defeated the state Labor government.

Nurses' militancy stemmed from two different kinds of experiences. The first was of working within the system, taking part in government reviews, lobbying and having high level meetings with the health minister – and getting nowhere. Hospital waiting lists in Victoria reached 27,000 before the strike, and the Labor government under Premier John Cain had cut the health budget, in real terms, every year since 1982-83. The toll on nurses was disastrous: they topped the 1986 compensation claims. In 1985, 10,000 left nursing, and a further 8,000 did not renew their practising certificates, leaving the state with a shortfall of about 14,000 nurses.

The second experience, over the decade or so before the strike, was of going outside the system and taking direct action.

A look at history

In April 1975, 4,000 angry nurses stormed the Victorian parliament. The issues were staffing and pay. They marched, singing 'We shall not be moved' and carrying placards saying 'Unite and Fight' and 'Dedication doesn't Pay the Rent'. Then, from 1977 to 1979, nurses in NSW and Queensland marched, picketed and imposed bans over staffing and bed closures. The action died down during 1980-81 but picked up again in 1982-83 with more strikes, bans and rallies, mostly in NSW. Most of the action was in response to state government attempts to cut back on health services by closing beds and holding down wages and condi-

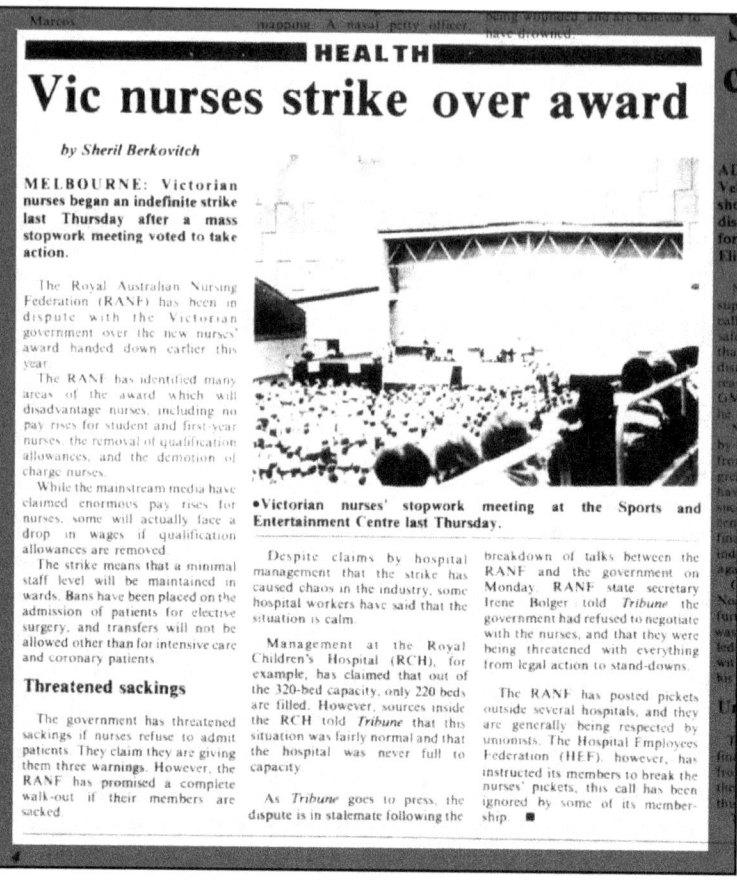

tions. In Sydney in 1982, nurses' action stopped the closure of some city hospitals. City workers, including builders' labourers, joined in the nurses' rallies against further closures.

Then, on 19 November 1983, NSW nurses went out on a total strike. One of them commented:

> Sydney Hospital was ready to go out in April 1982. Since then, there's been 18 months of discussion. The only way to prove anything to this geezer up in Parliament House is to withdraw our labour.[1]

The actions were possible because the NSW Nurses' Association and the Queensland Nurses' Association had both split from the Royal Australian Nurses' Federation (RANF) and had no clauses banning strikes. In all other states, the situation was quieter. The RANF still had a no-strike clause in its constitution – a relic of earlier days, when it was dominated by the matrons (later called directors of nursing). During the Depression, they had done things like petitioning the government for a 25 percent wage cut (and winning it) and continually lobbying for longer hours!

By 1982, fed up with this shackle, Victorian nurses decided to get rid of the clause. While the RANF was standing still, and nurses' wages and conditions were deteriorating, the Hospital Employees Federation (HEF) was taking action and winning wage rises for its nursing members. Nurses began to switch their allegiance to the HEF. One placard at the time summed up the situation: 'RANF just play the game, while the HEF strike and reap the gain.' It took until 1984 to dump the no-strike clause, but by then the decision was overwhelming.

Further strikes in NSW occurred in 1984 over a wages and hours claim, as the state government tried to trade off cuts in wages and conditions for a 38-hour week. Victorian nurses, faced with yet another cut in the health budget, fought the government in July 1984. The RANF explained: 'The 1.5% cuts are not the whole problem, they are the straw that broke the camel's back.' Members placed bans on non-nursing duties, and the government finally responded with an offer for 300 extra non-nursing staff. But there was a catch: the money to pay their wages was to come from nursing funds, so there would be an effective cut in nursing staff. Backed by the HEF, the RANF kept the bans on, and the government backed down and unconditionally offered 700 non-nursing staff by June 1985.

NSW nurses were still fighting the Wran government over their 38-hour week. They finally won in May 1986, but not without some determined action. For Victorian nurses, 1985 culminated in their first statewide strike.

Coupled with the cuts in health spending and inevitable staff shortages were some other changes in nursing. The introduction of new technology actually

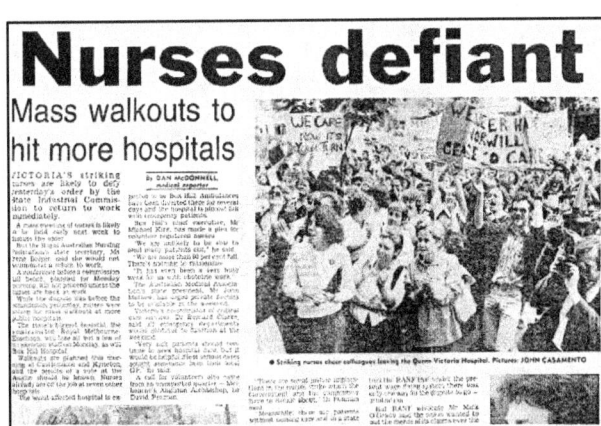

Nurses defy Industrial Relations Commission order to return to work

meant that more staff were required to run the newly created, highly specialised nursing units. Another consequence was that patients spent less time in hospital; with a higher turnover of patients came more work in admissions and discharge procedures. The higher turnover also created more stress in nurse-patient relations, with more people to relate to and less time to do it in. Without doubt, it was an explosive situation. But the government, as before, relied on nurses' dedication and did not heed the changing times.

By September 1985, nurses had had enough. Because they were still led by the old guard, the response began slowly. A night time mass meeting on 23 September attracted 1,700 members and adopted a log of claims for wage rises and improved conditions, including staff-patient ratios. Bans on wearing uniform and the use of agency staff were to be in force from 30 September. In the second week of October, nurses were to implement the RANF (and award) staff-patient ratio. A stopwork meeting was planned, but not until mid-October. However, hospitals were encouraged to hold their own stopwork meetings to discuss implementing the bans. The most important indication from the members that they meant business this time was the narrow defeat of a motion calling for immediate rolling strikes.

Health Minister David White responded on 30 September with an offer on wages and conditions. The proposed wage rise was to be phased in over three years and was well below what the union wanted. There was also the added rider: sign a three-year no-strike clause *and* increase productivity. The union rejected the offer and kept up the pressure.

After the nurses began working to the RANF staff-patient ratio from 7 October, White retaliated by directing management at the Alfred Hospital to scab. Management complied. Much to the government's fury, nurses at the hospital staged an immediate 24-hour walkout. Industrial Relations Minister Steve Crabb fumed: 'It's outrageous. I've never had a strike pulled on me in the middle of

Nurses rally outside office of Health Minister David White after mass meeting and march 17 October 1985

negotiations.'² But the nurses were even angrier: on 11 October, they agreed to an indefinite strike from the following Thursday, 17 October. After voting for the strike, thousands took to the streets and rallied outside White's office. RANF secretary Barbara Carson warned: 'I think the government has been indifferent to the RANF and the nurses have said, "Here's what we feel about that."'³

Negotiations continued, but with no progress. So, from 17 October, nurses across the state walked, leaving only skeleton staffing behind. They picketed hospitals, handed out leaflets to passers-by and collected money. The general feeling was that it was now or never. Most had never been on strike before, and the media called them industrially naïve, but it was quite the contrary. Wendy, a student nurse at the Royal Melbourne Hospital, explained:

> Nurses' conditions were so bad because people haven't fought to change them. But now nurses have changed. In the strike they're learning a lot about government tactics and union power.⁴

David White and the media claimed that patients would die and accompanied their misinformation campaign with threats to hold up the national wage case. They did not intimidate the strikers. 'Patients' lives were endangered before all of this,' said another Royal Melbourne student. 'There was no proper care because of lack of staff and supervision.' A placard: 'Overworked nurses: undercared-for patients' said it all.⁵

This time, the HEF officials did not back the strike. However, rank and file workers at many hospitals were openly supportive. HEF members at Prince Henry's met and voted not to cross picket lines. Unfortunately, the nurses didn't set them up, precisely for that reason.

The strike ended after five days with only a partial victory. The government's offer on staffing ratios was vague, but they did agree to cooperate with the RANF on admissions and discharges. Lower level nurses would get no increases; they would have to wait for arbitration. A number of nurses at the final mass meeting called this a sellout; they did not share the officials' confidence in 'neutral umpires'. But the main thing was that they had learned to strike. They would put this experience to good use in 1986.

Build-up to confrontation

The year 1986 began quietly, but there were a few rumblings. In February, Traralgon nurses struck over staff shortages but were sold out by the combined efforts of the RANF and Trades Hall Council leadership. Later, in an ill-considered measure, the Cain government took steps to recruit hundreds of English and Irish nurses at a cost of $6 million. White swept aside RANF fears that this would mean that the government would not tackle such issues as pay, child care, car parking and security. Then, when the government did delay, the union decided to take action over the overseas recruitment. They imposed bans on taking nurses from England and presented the government with a list of demands about their employment.

In a further attempt to paper over the growing cracks in the system, the government set up working parties at two of the worst-affected hospitals, Royal Melbourne and the Alfred, to recommend ways of improving working conditions. However, individual hospitals could not resolve the real issues – staffing and wages – and so the proposed changes were bound to have little or no impact. *The Age* later commented:

> The message in most public hospital annual reports is the same: 1985–86 was a disaster in terms of the number of patients treated, industrial relations, staff morale and finances. The reports...directly or indirectly express anger at the State government's health priorities, detail the effects of bed closures, spell out the cuts forced on services.[6]

Most nurses were still pinning their hopes on the state Industrial Relations Commission (IRC) hearings on wages and career structures, which had resulted from their industrial action in October 1985. On 20 June, they apparently got what they wanted: wage rises through a changed career structure. There were, however, two immediate problems. Firstly, the bulk of nurses, trainee and first year graduate nurses, would get nothing. Secondly, White seemed to be shifting his position on backdating. According to the *Financial Review*, the government and the IRC believed that the RANF 'would be obliged to accept such a generous decision even though its more junior members got nothing out of it.'[7] Nurses and their newly elected militant leader, Irene Bolger, thought differently.

Within five days of the decision, the union and the government were on a collision course. The issue was backdating pay rises. The private hospitals refused to pay up, so RANF members across the state imposed bans. White then threatened not to backdate state-employed nurses' pay unless they stopped their campaign; but Irene Bolger refused to back down: 'I can't give any commitment which would be selling my members down the drain.'

Facing continuing bans and RANF threats to strike, the government retreated by the end of the month. But, three days into July, the RANF and the government were back in the IRC over differences in the reclassification and qualification allowances. Under the June agreement, the RANF and hospitals had to make submissions to the Health Department outlining their proposals for the coverage of each of the new grades. It became clear at this stage that the government intended placing most nurses on the lowest grades. One of the picketers at Preston and Northcote Hospital (PANCH), who had 16 years' experience along with three certificates and was in the process of completing a university degree, suddenly found herself classed at the lowest Grade One level. Her story was repeated across the state.

The second problem was with qualification allowances. Even before the June agreement was reached, RANF organiser John Kotsifas was warning that the government intended cutting out the qualification allowance (extra payments for skills gained with special training certificates). The government and Health Department continued to deny this; but, as soon as the June agreement was made, qualification allowances were cut at a number of hospitals. This meant an overall pay cut for many nurses. Some were also demoted. So, within days of lifting the bans on elective surgery, nurses at four major hospitals reimposed them. By the end of July, bans were on in six hospitals, and there was again talk of strike action. Bolger warned that nurses were increasingly frustrated about the delays.

Then the IRC dropped its bombshell: on 7 August, it formally abolished the qualification allowance. 'We put in for a wage rise,' said one organiser, 'and we got a wage cut.' White published figures purporting to show that no nurse would lose money, but RANF members knew differently. In fact, one hospital had even backdated the cuts to 1 January and was demanding repayment.

A stopwork meeting on 14 August was angry, but still the nurses held back on strike action. Bans on elective admissions and wearing uniforms, operative from 20 August, were still the strategy. The meeting did endorse a log of claims which included pay rises for junior nurses. Nurses at two hospitals, the Alfred and the Austin, imposed additional bans on overseas recruits. Tension was rising. Newspaper editorials thundered that nurses could not be allowed the right to decide on patient admissions. Finally, management began standing nurses down, despite the fact that there was no standdown clause in the award. The IRC threatened not to pass on the 2.3 percent national wage rise while they were taking industrial action.

The bans remained. By 29 August, 78 nurses had been stood down. However, they did not just meekly accept the standdowns. Where they could, they kept working or took management on. At the Eye and Ear Hospital, many called in sick the day after a union delegate was stood down. Management had to close three wards and run others themselves. At Leongatha, nurses took a tea break following a standdown and did not return until the manager reconsidered his decision. At the Austin, three managers tried to stand over nurses; but, in the first ward they entered, RANF members formed a human barricade around a colleague targeted for a standdown. The angriest reaction came from St Vincent's, where 150 resigned in response to eight standdowns.

Two weeks after putting the bans on, nurses held another stopwork meeting, and 3,500 resolved to maintain the bans until the employers agreed to their claims. The resolution also demanded immediate reinstatement, without loss of pay or privileges, for all those stood down. Motions calling for White's resignation; for mass resignations; and for 24 and 48-hour strikes were put, but defeated. Nurses still weren't ready for all-out strike action. However, after the mass meeting, nurses at eight metropolitan hospitals began their own discussions of the mass resignation tactic.

In the face of the nurses' determination, the government and the IRC agreed to pay nurses who had been stood down. At a 5 September mass meeting, the union leaders then recommended lifting the bans. Negotiations resumed. The talks dragged on through September and into the following month, finally collapsing on 24 October. White and the Health Department were determined to downgrade most staff in order to contain the wages bill. The RANF was just as determined to win wage rises.

The strike begins

Trying to work within the system finally ended when 5,000 nurses thronged to a 31 October stopwork, overwhelmingly endorsing a rank and file motion to go out indefinitely. Critical care units were still staffed, and all wards had skeleton staff. A nurse from PANCH said: 'We had to do something, the government just keeps breaking promises.'[8] Calls for a total walkout were defeated, but nurses reinforced their message with a noisy march through the city.

The next day, 1 November, most metropolitan hospitals were picketed – although, for the first days, no goods were stopped. On the picket lines, nurses met many wellwishers. Encouragement to 'toot in support' resulted in continuous honking of car horns outside hospitals. Food, firewood and money poured in, and letters and telegrams backing the RANF overloaded Australia Post's deliveries to RANF headquarters in St Kilda. Workplace meetings and collections took place across Victoria and interstate, with sup-

port coming from blue and white-collar unions as well as from many rank and file HEF members.

The strike itself, while not completely in the hands of the rank and file, was often effectively run by the militants. When the people taking the action are the ones planning strike tactics, it strengthens their resolve. The strike committee met daily at the RANF offices to work out tactics and go over experiences. To ensure that members and other workers got the facts regularly, the union ran a program on community radio station 3CR and put out a daily strike bulletin. To maintain morale and solidarity, the strikers held regular picket line barbeques and sporting competitions, as well as fundraisers and an occasional champagne breakfast. Groups of nurses toured the country regions every day, building sup-

Striking nurses rally and picket

port and keeping country members informed. The RANF representative at Wimmera Base Hospital commented: 'I've never seen nurses so united and strong.'[9]

Unlike many other union leaderships, the RANF leaders backed rank and file decisions. The delegate at Epworth Hospital said: 'Irene is our employee. We tell her what to do.' Nicola, a first year graduate at Western General, related an experience from earlier in the dispute:

> Two months ago we decided on mass resignations. Irene thought it wasn't a particularly good strategy. But we did it anyway. After we went to her she said she'd support us 100%.

As a result of this commitment to carrying out decisions of the rank and file, Irene Bolger got standing ovations at most of the mass meetings.[10]

Nurses faced multiple personal traumas. Many cried as they walked out, and many had nightmares afterwards. Often, when they were on the picket line, they'd slip in the back way to visit patients they'd nursed. A charge sister remarked: 'It's been horrible for the past twelve months, but I think unity has come out of it.'[11]

The government refused to budge for weeks. Cain threatened the union with everything from manslaughter charges to deregistration and the *Essential Services Act* – threats which couldn't be disregarded, because his government had joined in such moves to deregister and destroy the militant BLF. The main concern behind the bluster and intimidation was maintaining the constraints of arbitration and the ALP-ACTU Accord. Cain and White weren't primarily afraid of the financial cost of an RANF victory; it was the political cost of any agreement reached after direct union action outside the system that made them so intransigent. Ken Howard, a federal RANF industrial officer, explained:

> A breakthrough by the nurses, or rather a breakout from the straitjacket of the arbitration system and the Accord would have had tremendous significance for all workers.[12]

Because the government wouldn't negotiate, nurses started to escalate the action. From 1 November, they walked out of all but critical care wards, hospital by hospital. Pickets began to stop non-essential supplies to the wards, and TWU drivers backed them. Cain responded by announcing that police would be used to break the pickets.

While relations between the RANF and HEF at some hospitals were good, with strong rank and file support, the HEF leadership publicly sided with the government. Secretary Les Butler instructed his members to cross picket lines. At hospitals like the Royal Melbourne, most of the members did; but at Prince Henry's, Queen Victoria and Western General, among others, they refused. HEF meetings at Prince Henry's agreed not to touch any goods brought in by scabs. Members threatened a total walkout if police intervened. If anything, according to Les Taylor, the HEF chief shop steward, the strike brought the two unions even closer at this hospital.

The Trades Hall Council leadership played as despicable a role as the HEF officials. Secretary Peter Marsh began by claiming that he didn't want to take responsibility for assisting the strike because it affected the health industry. That didn't stop him from trying the very next day to force the RANF to hand over the dispute to Trades Hall. He patronisingly told nurses that they needed help because they could no longer handle the dispute. Louise Ajani, from Western General, retorted: 'basically we don't think Trades Hall are acting in our interests.'[13] Fifteen hundred strikers personally delivered that message to Trades Hall at a rally on 7 November. Chanting 'No Trades Hall Interference!', a contingent stormed a health unions' meeting and saw to it that delegates voted against the intervention and supported the nurses.

By 19 November, 40 hospitals were hit by the strike, and building unions were threatening to impose bans. The IRC finally backed down from its refusal to arbitrate while the nurses were still out, calling private talks with all parties on 21 November.

It was to no avail. The government believed that the nurses would go back, and they were hoping that ACTU intervention would put them in their place.

The RANF Federal Council rejected ACTU control, although talks continued between the two organisations. The ACTU, while supporting the nurses' claims 'in principle', tried its best to undermine their position in practice. Its president, Simon Crean, personally attacked the union for its action on several occasions. He accused them of 'demanding more than was justified' and told them that they should return to work. Irene Bolger hit back with the blunt reply: 'Simon Crean should keep his mouth shut. He doesn't know what is going on.'[14]

On 8 December, the RANF again escalated the action. Nurses began walking out of critical care wards. This latest move was based partly on nurses' own demands and partly on a similar experience in Canada, which had brought the government to the negotiating table in seven minutes. However, it was not so easy in Victoria. Unlike the Canadian action, the Victorian walkout didn't involve all hospitals. Even by this stage, 50 per cent of hospital beds were still available, mostly through the private hospital system. And it was here that an important weakness emerged in the union's industrial campaign.

Fresh from the daily picket line reps' meeting, the member at PANCH announced the walkout. But, when asked what nurses were going to do if the government didn't respond, she replied: 'Not work? It *has* to work.' Having played their trump card, they had no strategy to continue building the strike if it failed.

And the government did refuse to negotiate, even after nurses left critical care wards. In fact, three days later, White escalated the dispute by announcing that the government would instruct State Enrolled Nurses (SENs) to do the nurses' work. The necessary legislation would be rushed through parliament. In this, the leaderships of the Australian Medical Association and the HEF assisted him. Les Butler of the HEF had no objection to his members doing work usually carried out by RANF members: 'As far as we are concerned it should have been done yesterday.'[15]

However, this time, the government had finally overstepped the mark. The RANF called national meetings to plan action over the use of SENs, with support likely from the more militant NSW and Queensland associations. Butler would probably also have been faced with widespread refusal by SENs, led by hospitals like Prince Henry's, to scab. Queen Victoria HEF members had already openly refused to obey union directives on the picket line, and there was flak from the union's interstate branches. In the Australian Capital Territory (ACT), for example, the HEF had joined forces with the RANF over staffing and wage demands and had publicly supported the Victorian RANF from the beginning. An important, but little-publicised, factor was that SENs, in a reversal of previous trends, had begun to leave the HEF and join the RANF. They were actually out on strike themselves.

While the Cain government did not publicly back down on the SENs until 17 December, the only real weapon it now had left was the ACTU. With the IRC opening up a loophole for ACTU intervention, the government was able to manoeuvre itself out of its dead-end position. After lengthy discussions, the RANF and ACTU finally agreed on a joint case to be put to the Commission on 15 December. The RANF had made some concessions, but the ACTU had agreed to all its major claims. Or, at least, that's what they told the union. But, when presenting the case, the ACTU's Jenny Acton started backtracking. When Irene Bolger tried to stop her, she accused the RANF of being 'unable to understand the difference between substantial and total agreement'. But RANF members and their leadership understood the ACTU's treachery only too well. Irene Bolger reported to that afternoon's stopwork: 'There is nothing joint about the proposal – it is now just the ACTU proposal. I think we have been sold out.' The nurses stayed out. The ACTU got the message, changing its position to one of total agreement with the RANF.[16]

Two days before the strike ended, White publicly withdrew the threat to use SENs. The RANF sent its members back to the critical care wards. Still, the government wouldn't agree to the RANF–ACTU package. Irene Bolger held firm:

> It's not enough for an agreement in principle because we don't trust him [David White] and our members don't trust him. He needs to agree to the whole package.[17]

Finally, on 19 December, on behalf of the Cain government, White agreed to the 'whole package', and the nurses went back. A week later, *The Australian* said of the nurses' victory:

> Despite all the posturing...the nurses did prove themselves strong enough industrially to make significant gains. It took five weeks of strike, but the government did finally agree its $54.7m allocation under the June award was insufficient.[18]

Some issues

The nurses' strike stood out as a victory in a time of working class defeat. Union organisation had been destroyed at Robe River, at Mudginberri and in the Queensland power industry. State and federal Labor governments, along with the ACTU leadership, were in the process of smashing the militant BLF. The nurses showed that it was still possible to win.

The Hawke government had come to power on the basis of its Accord with the union bureaucracy. Although they presented the Accord as a program in the interests of workers, in practice, it was designed to cut wages and boost company profits while making it harder for unionists to fight back. At the same time, Labor governments at both state and federal levels were carrying out budget cuts. As part of this, health spending in Victoria had been cut in real terms every year since 1982-83. A building worker from the Riverside Quay construction site commented: 'Cain spent $40 million to destroy the BLF. He should have used it to fix up the hospital system.'[19]

The government planned to cut bed numbers, pushing more people into the private health system. It also planned to restructure the nursing profession in ways that would cut costs at workers' expense and make union organisation more difficult. In other words, the nurses were facing a very determined opponent. There was also strong speculation among informed participants that the HEF had given the government some sort of promise to undermine the nurses in exchange for increased coverage. The HEF leaders were worried that they might be next in line for deregistration after the BLF, and it is possible that some agreement on this issue was reached too.

Yet, the nurses succeeded, and that boosted other workers' confidence. They gave the IRC short shrift – a lesson also not lost on other unionists. Irene Bolger commented that most nurses considered it 'a bit of a kangaroo court', and the nurses forced the Commission to back down on every issue. They also exposed the ACTU's double-dealing and forced it to support them.

The strike also challenged conventional ideas among the nurses themselves. For example, they had generally accepted what the media said about the BLF, even after the RANF began to get some of the same treatment. Some of them even asked

Striking nurses' street rally.

BLF members to leave one rally. But, as BLF members continued to support the pickets and the strike, attitudes began to change. A nurse at the Queen Victoria said:

> I feel so guilty. I never supported the BLF. I never went and talked to anyone about what was going on. I just believed what I read.[20]

Nurses initially had faith in the police, and the police did their best to encourage this faith. Commissioner Mick Miller even told White not to count on police to break the pickets. But the pretence ended about halfway through the dispute. Without warning, 50 police dragged picketers at the Royal Melbourne across a gravel roadway, bruising and choking them. Twice, they escorted linen vans through the picket. The government probably hoped that this would demoralise the strikers just before a key mass meeting. It failed, but it showed where the police stood in a crunch.

Arguments about losing public support are often used to discourage public sector workers from taking industrial action. Nurses are a prime target. Throughout their strike, however, despite government and media attacks, public support for the RANF stayed around 75–80 percent. When they finally walked out of critical care, public opinion appeared to shift somewhat. But, accord-

ing to Bolger, the support for their demands was still solid. More people simply thought that they should return to work *and* that the government should give them what they wanted.

Among nurses themselves, the benefits of unionism became clearer. Union membership climbed steadily during the dispute. One organiser quipped: 'Every time David White opens his mouth, another 200 nurses join the RANF.' But it was mainly the union's own actions that won their allegiance. Julie Watts, from St Vincent's, said: 'It's terrific really. I feel very strongly that this is the best move nurses have made for their profession and health care.'[21] As well as laying to rest the bogey of public opinion, the dispute also put another nail in the coffin of the myth of women's passivity. The *Sun* reported:

> As if anyone needed further proof of the radicalization of Florence Nightingale there it was at Olympic Park yesterday – a T-shirt pledging allegiance to 'Irene Bolger's Nurses' Liberation Front'. Even among the

poor pun placards attacking 'White Lies' and 'White Slavery' and the buoyant almost pep rally atmosphere of the packed mass meeting, there was little doubt the striking nurses were going to hang tough. At times, between the laughter and cheering, you could even hear talk of solidarity and the workers' struggle.[22]

Newspapers commented that no male unionist would have been subject to the same campaign of innuendo and smear tactics, implying that all the attacks on Irene Bolger were sexist. While there was a sexist edge to some of the abuse, militant unionists were actually being subjected to equally savage attacks, especially on the BLF.

A number of union leaderships held back from supporting the strike because of their allegiance to the ALP-ACTU Accord. The Accord meant demobilising the union ranks. If they called action in support of the RANF, union officials might find their members asking: if we can strike for the nurses, why not strike for our own demands?

While the union officials held back, their members often showed great enthusiasm for the nurses' cause. Employees at the Ford Broadmeadows car plant said that, if the nurses in the medical centre set up a picket line, they wouldn't cross it. Latrobe Valley power workers threatened to pull the plug on the state's electricity supply, and 17 local union branches met to discuss action, but the union leadership headed them off. Electricians banned work on hospital lifts, while building workers and wharfies levied themselves and held workplace meetings. They also held a one-day stoppage and marched through the city. TWU members refused to cross picket lines, and 1,000 unionists braved a torrential downpour to attend a lunchtime solidarity rally. Many others collected money, visited picket lines and delivered food. Had the RANF called openly for solidarity action, these individual and sometimes spontaneous actions could have been turned into a mass solidarity movement.

The key to this would have been the HEF, whose members were used to break picket lines for linen and coal delivery. Because the HEF continued to work on the wards and work with 'volunteers', the hospital could continue functioning. There were strong indications that rank and file HEF members at a number of hospitals would have been prepared to defy their leadership and walk out in support of the nurses. At Prince Henry's, they offered support from the beginning. Les Taylor, chief HEF shop steward, said that his members: 'wanted to take more action than they did. If the RANF branch in the hospital had approached us we would have taken direct action.'[23]

Taylor indicated that several other hospitals would have gone out as well. While admitting that it would have been hard to build up from there, he thought that HEF support would have brought the government to the negotiating table much sooner. It would also have built up solidarity at the rank and file level between the two unions, whose relations had been bitter at many hospitals. As the response from other unions to the attempted use of paid 'volunteers' (strikebreakers) indicated, the nurses could have called for more militant action from other hospital workers. Nurses in other states could also have been approached to take solidarity action. As it was, interstate nurses were only asked to give money.

Irene Bolger later argued that spreading the dispute was 'not feasible' and that the Victorian branch had no option but to go it alone. Certainly, there would have been difficulties. The fragmented nature of the union militated against it, and the Accord had undermined traditions of union solidarity. NSW nurses received a relatively generous pay rise during the Victorian dispute – a move surely calculated to stem any support for the Victorian nurses and to bolster the right-wing executive of the NSW branch. Even so, Victorian RANF members could have toured interstate and laid the basis for support action. Touring country regions of their own state had been important in building support.

Despite the problems, the nurses' strike showed the power of solidarity at the rank and file level, not only among the strikers but in the working class as a whole. It showed how a predominantly female group of workers could sustain mass industrial action and give a lead to other workers of both sexes. Their story, like those of the other rebel women who appear in this book, offers an inspiring alternative to conventional women's history.

Acronyms and Abbreviations

ACT	Australian Capital Territory
ACTU	Australian Council of Trade Unions
AEU	Amalgamated Engineering Union
AISF	Australian Insurance Staffs' Federation
ALP	Australian Labor Party
AMA	Amalgamated Miners' Association
ASE	Australasian Society of Engineers
AWA	Amalgamated Wireless (Australasia)
AWM	Australian Woollen Mills
BLF	Builders' Labourers' Federation
CPA	Communist Party of Australia
CTU	Clothing Trades Union
FE	Federal Executive
FIA	Federated Ironworkers' Association
HEF	Hospital Employees Federation
IEIA	Insurance Employers' Industrial Association
IRC	Industrial Relations Commission
IS	International Socialists
IWD	International Women's Day
LVA	Labour Volunteer Army
MIC	Militant Insurance Clerks
MM	Minority Movement
NHA	New Housewives' Association
NSW	New South Wales
PANCH	Preston and Northcote Hospital

RANF	Royal Australian Nurses' Federation
SEN	State Enrolled Nurses
SMWIU	Sheet Metal Workers' Industrial Union
SRC	Staffs' Reference Committee
TWU	Transport Workers' Union
UAW	Union of Australian Women
UGRM	Unemployed Girls' Relief Movement
UWM	Unemployed Workers' Movement
VTEB	Victorian Turkish Workers Association
WEB	Women's Employment Board

Endnotes

Preface

1   Both quotes taken from Emma Sleath, 'Key moment in Australia's union history commemorated', ABC Local, 20 April 2009, https://www.abc.net.au/local/stories/2009/04/20/2546761.htm [audio file].

Introduction to Third Edition

1   'Glen Tomasetti', The Australian Women's Register, https://www.womenaustralia.info/biogs/AWE0600b.htm.
2   *Melbourne Sun*, 12 November 1986.
3   Kath Larkin, Belle Gibson, 2022, personal communications.
4   Kath Larkin, 'The Kortex strike'. Marxism Conference, 2021, https://marxtalks.com.au/talk/migrant-women-fight-back-the-1981-melbourne-kortex-strike. The following quotes are from this talk and interviews with Bahriye Akalin in 2020.
5   Alec Kahn, 'Nurses' strike: Sisters are doing it for themselves – and us', *Socialist Action*, December 1986, p. 3.
6   Liz Ross, *Stuff the Accord! Pay Up! Workers' Resistance to the ALP–ACTU Accord*, Melbourne, Interventions, 2020.
7   Catherine Robertson, '"We're not pussycats!" Country Road warehouse workers strike', *Red Flag*, 21 November 2021.

Introduction to 1998 edition

1. Quoted in Alex Callinicos, *The Revolutionary Ideas of Marx*, London, Bookmarks, 1983, p. 80.
2. R. H. B. Kearns, *Broken Hill: A Pictorial History*, Adelaide, Investigator, 1982.
3. This is based on conversations with trade unionists in Broken Hill.
4. For a contemporary analysis, see Tom Bramble, 'Managers of Discontent: Problems With Labour Leadership', in Rick Kuhn and Tom O'Lincoln (eds.), *Class & Class Conflict in Australia*, Melbourne, Longman, 1996.
5. Janey Stone, 'Brazen Hussies and God's Police: Feminist Historiography and the Great Depression', *Hecate*, vol. VIII, no. 1, 1982, p. 21.
6. As evidenced in Terry Irving (ed.), *Challenges to Labour History*, Sydney, University of NSW Press, 1994.
7. Marilyn Lake, 'The Politics of Respectability: Identifying the Masculinist Context', *Historical Studies*, vol. 22, no. 86, April 1986, p. 116; and 'The Constitution of Political Subjectivity', in Irving, *Challenges to Labour History*, p. 86.
8. Stone, 'Brazen Hussies', p. 20.
9. *Barrier Miner*, 8 December 1906.
10. Joy Damousi, *Women Come Rally: Socialism, Communism and Gender in Australia 1890-1955*, Melbourne, Oxford University Press, 1994, pp. 5, 17.
11. *Barrier Truth*, 11 December 1908, *Barrier Miner*, 11 December 1908.
12. Joy Damousi, *Women Come Rally*, pp. 16-17.
13. Marilyn Lake, 'The Politics of Respectability', p. 116.
14. Patricia Grimshaw, Marilyn Lake, Ann McGrath and Marian Quartly, *Creating a Nation*, Melbourne, McPhee Gribble, 1994, pp. 151-203.
15. Marilyn Lake, 'The Constitution of Political Subjectivity', pp. 84-85.
16. Terry Irving, 'Introduction', in Irving, *Challenges to Labour History*, p. 16

1. Militant Spirits

1. *Silver Age*, 26 August 1892.
2. *Barrier Miner*, 4 July 1892.
3. *Barrier Miner*, 22, 24 and 25 August 1892.
4. *Silver Age*, 26 August 1892; *Leader*, 3 September 1892; *Silver Age*, 26 Au-

	gust 1892; *Barrier Miner*, 25 August 1892.
5	*Barrier Miner*, 1 September 1892.
6	*Barrier Truth*, 16 October 1908.
7	*Barrier Truth*, 2 October 1908; 23 October 1908.
8	*Barrier Daily Truth*, 2, 5 and 6 January 1909.
9	*Barrier Daily Truth*, 11 January 1909.
10	George Dale, *The Industrial History of Broken Hill*, Melbourne, Fraser & Jenkinson, 1918, pp. 118-119; *Barrier Daily Truth*, 1 and 4 February 1909; *Barrier Miner*, 27 April 1909.
11	*Barrier Daily Truth*, 4 February 1909.
12	*Barrier Daily Truth*, 17 and 23 July 1916; George Dale, *The Industrial History of Broken Hill*, p. 207; Brian Kennedy, *Silver, Sin and Sixpenny Ale: A Social History of Broken Hill*, 1883-1921, Melbourne University Press, 1978, p. 139.
13	*Barrier Daily Truth*, 10 August 1916.
14	*Barrier Daily Truth*, 30 October 1916; Kennedy, *Silver, Sin and Sixpenny Ale*, p. 140.
15	Australian Archives (ACT): A3932/1; SC294; Bolshevism, Sedition and Disloyalty. Australian Archives (ACT): A6122/40; iii; Summary of Communism.
16	Dale, *The Industrial History of Broken Hill*, p. 223.
17	Kennedy, *Silver, Sin and Sixpenny Ale*, p. 88.
18	*Flame*, November 1906.
19	Joy Damousi, *Women Come Rally: Socialism, Communism and Gender in Australia, 1890-1955*, Melbourne, Oxford University Press, 1994, p. 36; *Barrier Daily Truth*, 22 March 1907; 28 September 1916.
20	*Barrier Truth*, 16 October 1908; 23 October 1908.
21	*Barrier Truth*, 7 December 1906; 14 December 1906; *Barrier Miner*, 7-14 December 1906; *Flame*, December 1906.
22	*Barrier Truth*, 20 October 1908.
23	Alan Katen Dunstan, *'Broke-N-Ill The Writing On the Wall': Cartoons From Around the 'Lock-Out' 1909-1910*, Broken Hill City Council, 1994, Plate 22.
24	Kennedy, *Silver, Sin and Sixpenny Ale*, p. 96; *Barrier Daily Truth*, 27 March 1909; Tom Mann, *Socialism*, Melbourne, Tocsin, 1905, p. 58; *Barrier Miner*, 27 March 1909; *Barrier Daily Truth*, 31 July 1916; 21 August 1916.
25	*Silver Age*, 26 August 1892.

26   *Barrier Miner*, 25 August 1892.
27   *Barrier Miner*, 26 August 1892; 10 September 1892; 15 September 1892.
28   *Silver Age*, 25 August 1892. The kingdom of Dahomey, on the west coast of Africa in the late nineteenth century, had an all female army, which Europeans referred to as 'Dahomey Amazons'.
29   *Barrier Miner*, 1 May 1909.
30   Australian Archives (ACT): A6122/40; iii; Review of Communism.
31   *Barrier Daily Truth*, 9 October 1916.
32   Joy Damousi, 'Socialist Women and Gendered Space: The Anti-Conscription and Anti-War Campaigns of 1914–1918', *Labour History*, no. 60, May 1991, p. 5.
33   *Barrier Daily Truth*, 28 August 1916.
34   *Barrier Daily Truth*, 11 September 1916.
35   Joy Damousi, *Women Come Rally*, pp. 34–35, 51.
36   *Flame*, January 1908.
37   *Barrier Miner*, 12 October 1908.
38   *Barrier Truth*, 16 October 1908.
39   *Barrier Truth*, 20 October 1908.
40   Joy Damousi, *Women Come Rally*, pp. 35–36. Her argument is based on theoretical analysis ranging from an examination of English middle-class life 1780–1850 to gender in Marakwet society in Kenya, rather than any evidence from the Australian workers' movement itself. Joy Damousi, 'Socialist Women and Gendered Space', p. 5.
41   *Flame*, June 1906.
42   *Barrier Miner*, 20 August 1892.
43   *Barrier Miner*, 20 March 1909.
44   Judith Allen, '"Our Deeply Degraded Sex" and "The Animal in Man": Rose Scott, Feminism and Sexuality 1890–1925', *Australian Feminist Studies*, nos. 7 & 8, Summer, 1988, pp. 71–73; Darryn Kruse and Charles Sowerwine, 'Feminism and Pacifism: "Woman's Sphere" in Peace and War', in Norma Grieve and Ailsa Burns (eds.), *Australian Women: New Feminist Perspectives*, Melbourne, Oxford University Press, 1986, p. 42.
45   Verity Burgmann makes a similar point with regard to the image, style and language of the Industrial Workers of the World in her *Revolutionary Industrial Unionism: The Industrial Workers of the World in Australia*, Cambridge University Press, 1995, p. 110.
46   George Dale, *The Industrial History of Broken Hill*, p. 246.

2. Brazen hussies and God's police

1 Anne Summers, *Damned Whores and God's Police*, Ringwood, Penguin, 1975, p. 411.
2 Judy Mackinolty, 'Woman's Place...', in Judy Mackinolty (ed.), *The Wasted Years? Australia's Great Depression*, Sydney, Allen & Unwin, 1981, p. 110.
3 Margaret Power, 'Women and Economic Crises: the Great Depression and the Present Crisis', First Women and Labour Conference, 1978, separate paper, pp. 3-4.
4 Power, 'Women and Economic Crises', p. 2.
5 Jenny Bremner, 'Equal Status, Equal Pay and Equality of Opportunity: Muriel Heagney and the Status of Women in the Great Depression', Second Women and Labour Conference, 1980, p. 310.
6 Bremner, 'Equal Status', p. 309.
7 Dorothy Benjamin, 'The Discrimination Against Women and their Exploitation in the Clothing Trade During the Depression of 1929-36, and the Police Role of the Victorian Amalgamated Trades Union', Second Women and Labour Conference, 1980, pp. 316-326.
8 Quoted in Bremner, 'Equal Status', p. 309.
9 Benjamin, 'The Discrimination Against Women', p. 320; Bremner, 'Equal Status', p. 306.
10 See Tom O'Lincoln, *The Militant Minority: Organising Rank and File Workers in the Thirties*, Melbourne, Socialist Action, 1986.
11 Summers, *Damned Whores*, quote from p. 403.
12 Andree Wright, 'Jessie Street, Feminist', in Ann Curthoys, Susan Eade and Peter Spearrit (eds.), *Women at Work*, Canberra, Australian Society for the Study of Labour History, 1975, p. 62.
13 *Working Woman*, January 1936.
14 Megan McMurchy, Margot Oliver and Jeni Thornley, *For Love or Money: A Pictorial History of Women and Work in Australia*, Ringwood, Penguin, 1983, p. 85.
15 Summers, *Damned Whores*, p. 405.
16 Power, 'Women and Economic Crises', p. 3; Summers, *Damned Whores*, p. 404. Summers goes on: 'although some other women might have agreed with her in principle about women's right to economic independence, few were able or prepared to do much about it at a time like that. Most of them were too busy – helping their families survive or else en-

gaged in voluntary relief work'. But the 1930s feminists were not as isolated from potential support as many of today's feminists believe. The Unemployed Workers' Movement (UWM) held a conference in Sydney in July 1930, where women workers and workers' wives adopted these resolutions (*Working Woman*, August 1930):

- it is impossible adequately to deal with the unemployed without considering the special question of the unemployed working women;
- criticism of women's place in the home as a 'bourgeois illusion';
- criticism of the labour movement for not recognising that women have a permanent place in industry and for not organising them into trade unions;
- denounced all labour organisations denying women their rightful place and demanded women on all committees, demonstrations etc.;
- Demands included – unemployed women to receive wages for the period out of work; equal pay; an end to night work for women; maternity leave; day nurseries financed by a tax on capital and administered by 'working class organisations'.

The UWM and the MM held women's conferences at regular intervals for several years. Most of their demands would have been adopted under the influence of the Communist Party. One, in 1931, called for contraceptive information and legal abortion, while the MM's program included a demand for a fight against dismissals of married women and equal employment relief (*Working Woman*, January 1932; *Red Leader*, 29 June 1932).

17 Edna Ryan, interview 1981, quoted in McMurchy, Oliver and Thornley, *For Love or Money*, p. 96.

18 *Working Woman*, November 1930; September 1930. A CPA official wrote at the time: 'Of utmost importance in the strike was the prominence of women workers... Two women delegates sat on the Strike Council. Women engaged in the picketing.' Quoted in Jim Moss, *Representatives of Discontent: History of the Communist Party in South Australia 1921– 1981*, Melbourne, Communist and Labour Movement History Group, 1983, p. 22.

19 *Working Woman*, June 1932; December 1932.

20 *Working Woman*, January 1936.

21 *Working Woman*, May 1935.

22   Bessie, in 'Living It Up on the Dole', *Mabel*, June 1976.
23   Jim Munro, 'Communists and the Unemployed Workers Movement', *Sixty Years of Struggle: A Journal of Communist and Labour History*, vol. 2, Sydney, Red Pen, 1982, p. 47.
24   *Working Woman*, May 1935.
25   'Indignation', interview with Pat Hurd, in Kay Daniels and Mary Murnane (eds.), *Uphill All the Way*, University of Queensland Press, 1980, pp. 305-6.
26   Aida, in 'Living It Up on the Dole'.
27   Aida, in 'Living It Up on the Dole'.
28   *Working Woman*, February 1936.
29   Jean Devanny, *Sugar Heaven*, Melbourne, Redback Press, 1982. Devanny was a member of the CPA and wrote several novels.
30   Winifred Mitchell, 'Wives of the Radical Labour Movement', in Curthoys, Eade and Spearitt, *Women at Work*, p. 5; Winifred Mitchell, 'Women in Mining Communities', First Women and Labour Conference, 1978, extra papers, p. 4.
31   Grace Scanlon, in 'Women on the Coalfields', *Mabel*, March 1976.
32   Grace Scanlon, in 'Women on the Coalfields', *Mabel*, March 1976.
33   Grace Scanlon, in 'Women on the Coalfields', *Mabel*, March 1976. On a more recent instance of the transforming power of women's support for striking miners, see Janey Stone, '"Iron Ladies": Women in the 1984-5 British Miners' Strike', *Hecate*, vol. XI, no. 2, 1985.
34   Quoted in Mitchell, 'Wives of the Radical Labour Movement', p. 8.
35   Joyce Stevens, '"Without fear or favour" - Lucy Barnes', paper delivered to the First Women and Labour Conference, Macquarie University, May 1978, vol. 1, *Women and the Australian Labour Movement*, pp. 34-38.
36   *Red Leader*, 24 August 1932; 7 September 1932; *The Argus*, 11-26 August 1932; *Working Woman*, September 1932.
37   'Girl Textile Workers Warned By Police', *Sydney Morning Herald*, 10 January 1934, reproduced in McMurchy, Oliver and Thornley, *For Love or Money*, p. 104.
38   *Working Woman*, February and March 1934; *The Argus*, 12-30 January and 8-9 March 1934.
39   *The Argus*, January and February 1938.
40   Benjamin, 'The Discrimination Against Women', p. 323.
41   Benjamin, 'The Discrimination Against Women', p. 325; *The Argus*, 9, 14

	July 1932.
42	*The Argus*, 27 March 1935; 23 July 1936.
43	*The Argus*, 20 June 1930; 3, 5, 18 November 1937.
44	*The Argus*, 30 May 1939.
45	*The Argus*, May and July 1935; 14 May 1936.
46	*Working Woman*, October and November 1935; Flo Davis, 'Forty years organising', in *Sixty Years of Struggle*, vol. 1, p. 38; *The Argus*, 5 October 1937; *Sydney Morning Herald*, 14 November 1933.
47	Wright, 'Jessie Street, Feminist', p. 61.
48	Quoted in David Mitchell, *The Fighting Pankhursts*, New York, MacMillan, 1967, p. 219.
49	David Mitchell, *The Fighting Pankhursts*, p. 223; J. Castle, 'The Australian Women's Guild of Empire', First Women and Labour Conference, Macquarie University, 1978, separate paper, p. 3.
50	*Woman Worker*, October 1929; Castle, 'The Australian Women's Guild of Empire', p. 2. Alexandra Kollontai was a prominent Russian Communist.
51	Castle, 'The Australian Women's Guild of Empire', p. 7.
52	Peter Spearrit, 'Women in Sydney factories c 1920-50', in Curthoys, Eade and Spearitt, *Women at Work*, p. 54.
53	Castle, 'The Australian Women's Guild of Empire', p. 7.
54	*Working Woman*, May 1934.
55	David Mitchell, *The Fighting Pankhursts*, p. 223.
56	*The Argus*, 10 September 1931.

3. Class struggle on the home front

1	Judge Alfred Foster, chairman of the Women's Employment Board, quoted in Constance Larmour, 'Women's Wages and the WEB' in Curthoys, Eade and Spearritt, *Women at Work*, pp. 50-51.
2	'Beauty In War-time', *The Sun News-Pictorial*, Melbourne, 22 May 1940, reproduced in Andrew Bolt (ed.) *Our Home Front 1939-45*, Melbourne, Wilkinson Books, 1995, p. 39; *Australian Women's Weekly*, 5 July 1941, quoted in Andree Wright, 'The Women's Weekly: Depression and the War Years', *Refractory Girl*, no. 3, 1973, p. 11.
3	Quoted in Wright, 'The Women's Weekly', p. 12.
4	'Won't You Change Your Job For Me?' Recruitment poster, reproduced in Marian Aveling and Joy Damousi (eds.), *Stepping Out of History. Doc-

ENDNOTES

5   *uments of Women at Work in Australia*, North Sydney, Allen & Unwin, 1991, p. 141.
5   *Australian Women's Weekly*, 3 July 1943, quoted in Wright, 'The Women's Weekly', p. 12.
6   'More Than Duty', advertisement for Yardley, reproduced in *The Home Front Family Album: Remembering Australia 1939–1945*, Sydney, Weldon Publishing, 1991, p. 124.
7   'Eve in Overalls', *Ordnance News*, October 1943, p. 1.
8   *Australian Women's Weekly*, 25 August 1945, quoted in Wright, 'The Women's Weekly', p. 13.
9   Interestingly, it was an Anglican archbishop who pointed out the double standard operating: servicemen were excused for lapses in behaviour, while the sacrifices and contributions of factory workers were taken for granted, and they were expected to suffer hardships in silence. *The Home Front Family Album*, p. 120.
10   For example, Judge Foster of the WEB commented: 'In some cases, particularly on monotonous labour, managers have said that the women work better'. Quoted in Larmour, 'Women's Wages and the WEB', p. 51.
11   Quoted in Carmel Shute, 'From Balaclavas to Bayonets: Women's Voluntary War Work, 1939–41', *Hecate*, vol. VI, no. 1, 1980, p. 24.
12   Quoted in Robin Kramer, 'Female Employment During the Second World War', Third Women and Labour Conference, 1982, p. 457.
13   Quoted in Kate Darian-Smith, *On the Home Front: Melbourne in Wartime 1939–1945*, Oxford University Press, 1990, p. 59.
14   Edna Ryan and Anne Conlon, *Gentle Invaders: Australian Women at Work 1788–1974*, Sydney, Nelson, 1975, p. 112; Tom Sheridan, *Mindful Militants: The Amalgamated Engineering Union in Australia 1920–1927*, Cambridge University Press, 1975, p. 159.
15   Kramer, 'Female Employment During the Second World War', pp. 449–453; Charlie Fox, *Working in Australia*, Sydney, Allen & Unwin, 1991, p. 136.
16   Penny Ryan and Tim Rowse, 'Women, Arbitration and the Family', in Curthoys, Eade and Spearritt, *Women at Work*, p. 15; Larmour, 'Women's Wages and the WEB', p. 55; Kramer, 'Female Employment During the Second World War', p. 451.
17   Kramer, 'Female Employment During the Second World War', p. 453.
18   Larmour, 'Women's Wages and the WEB', p. 49.
19   Quoted in Judge Alfred Foster, 'The Experience of the Women's Employ-

20 Kramer, 'Female Employment During the Second World War', p. 454; Ryan and Conlon, *Gentle Invaders*, pp. 126, 137; Foster, 'The Experience of the Women's Employment Board in Australia', p. 633; Larmour, 'Women's Wages and the WEB', p. 49.
21 Quoted in Ryan and Conlan, *Gentle Invaders*, p. 129.
22 Lynn Beaton, 'The Importance of Women's Paid Labour – Based on the Study of Women at Work in the Second World War', Second Women and Labour Conference, 1980, p. 73.
23 On this dynamic, see Tom Bramble, 'Managers of Discontent: Problems With Labour Leadership', in Rick Kuhn and Tom O'Lincoln (eds.), *Class and Class Conflict in Australia*, Melbourne, Longman, 1996, pp. 40–57.
24 Ernie Thornton, *Trade Unions and the War*, Federal Council of the Federated Ironworkers' Association, 1942, p. 20.
25 Quoted in Darian-Smith, *On the Home Front*, p. 73.
26 One AEU official wrote: 'During the last war (in Britain) when women entered the metal trades in large numbers...engineers were inclined to regard the situation as abnormal and transitory, whilst the prevailing low rates for women's work did not conduce to their acceptance as fellow Unionists.' *Women in the Engineering Industry*, Amalgamated Engineering Union, May 1943, p. 4. Could the union actually have believed that women deliberately asked for low wages in order to avoid having to unionise?
27 Sheridan, *Mindful Militants*, p. 148.
28 Sheridan, *Mindful Militants*, p. 52.
29 *Women in the Engineering Industry*, p. 5.
30 Sheridan, *Mindful Militants*, p. 162.
31 Sheridan, *Mindful Militants*, pp. 152, 160.
32 James Jeffreys, 'The Story of the Engineers 1800–1945', in *The 25th Anniversary of the AEU, Australia*, Amalgamated Engineering Union, 1945, p. 260.
33 *Women in the Engineering Industry*, inside front cover; Sheridan, *Mindful Militants*, p. 160.
34 Sheridan, *Mindful Militants*, p. 163.
35 *The Sheet Metal Worker*, April 1940.
36 Bulletin produced by the Sheet Metal Workers' Union giving Federal Conference Report, April 1940; *The Sheet Metal Worker*, April 1941; December 1941.

37 *The Sheet Metal Worker*, April 1942.
38 *The Sheet Metal Worker*, August 1942; October 1942.
39 *The Sheet Metal Worker*, April 1944.
40 Joan Curlewis, 'Women Working in Heavy Industry in the Second World War', Third Women and Labour Conference, pp. 462–3; Interview with Rose (Muldoon) Cruickshank, in Curlewis, 'Women Working in Heavy Industry', p. 465; *The Sheet Metal Worker*, December 1942; February 1943; October 1943.
41 *The Sheet Metal Worker*, December 1942.
42 *The Sheet Metal Worker*, April 1943.
43 *The Sheet Metal Worker*, December 1943.
44 *The Sheet Metal Worker*, October 1943.
45 Quoted in Joyce Stevens, *Taking the Revolution Home: Work Among Women in the Communist Party of Australia 1920–1945*, Melbourne, Sybilla Press, 1987, p. 85.
46 In contrast to female wages, where employers fought tooth and nail against the WEB rulings and other increases, employers were happy to offer financial inducements to men, such as nominally transferring them to higher classifications. This they could do without affecting profit rates, because war contracts were determined on a cost-plus basis. Sheridan, *Mindful Militants*, pp. 151–2; Jack Hutson, *Six Wage Concepts*, Amalgamated Engineering Union, 1971, p. 115; *The Sheet Metal Worker*, August 1941.
47 Muriel Heagney, 'Women in the Engineering Industry', in *The 25th Anniversary of the AEU*, p. 54; Hutson, *Six Wage Concepts*, p. 115; Ryan and Rowse, 'Women, Arbitration and the Family', p. 25.
48 Hutson, *Six Wage Concepts*, p. 114; Ryan and Rowse, 'Women, Arbitration and the Family', p. 25.
49 Darian-Smith, *On the Home Front*, p. 63.
50 *The Sheet Metal Worker*, June 1943; October 1943; April 1944.
51 Heagney, 'Women in the Engineering Industry', p. 53.
52 *The Sheet Metal Worker*, February 1944; April 1945; August 1944; October 1944; 'Girls demand back pay', *Sydney Morning Herald*, 23 October 1942, reproduced in McMurchy, Oliver and Thornley, *For Love or Money*, p. 122.
53 Jessie Street, *Truth or Repose*, Sydney, Australasian Book Society, 1966, p. 216; Ryan and Rowse, 'Women, Arbitration and the Family', p. 25.
54 Interview with Rosemary (Archdeacon) Davies in Curlewis, 'Women

Working in Heavy Industry', p. 466.
55 *The Sheet Metal Worker,* June 1943; Curlewis, 'Women Working in Heavy Industry', p. 463.
56 Beaton, 'The Importance of Women's Paid Labour', p. 73.
57 Marilyn Lake, 'The War Over Women's Work', in Verity Burgmann and Jenny Lee (eds.), *A Most Valuable Acquisition: A People's History of Australia since 1788*, Penguin, 1988, p. 209; Ryan and Conlon, *Gentle Invaders*, p. 133.
58 Beaton, 'The Importance of Women's Paid Labour', p. 73.
59 'Textile Strike Affects 20,000', *The Sun News-Pictorial*, Melbourne, 9 September 1941, reproduced in Andrew Bolt (ed.), *Our Home Front*, p. 104.
60 Joyce Batterham, in Joyce Stevens, *Taking the Revolution Home*, p. 208.
61 Quoted in Peter Spearritt, 'Women in Sydney Factories 1920-50', in Curthoys, Eade and Spearritt, *Women at Work*, p. 45.
62 Betty Reilly, 'The Rag Trade', *Australian Left Review*, September 1982, p. 7; 'Textile Strike Extends', *Sydney Morning Herald*, 25 February 1943, reproduced in McMurchy, Oliver and Thornley, *For Love or Money*, p. 123; Betty Reilly, interview 1981, quoted in McMurchy, Oliver and Thornley, *For Love or Money*, p. 123.
63 McMurchy, Oliver and Thornley, *For Love or Money*, p. 113; '8000 To Leave Jobs', *Sydney Morning Herald*, 26 February 1943 and 'Idle Textile Factories', *Sydney Morning Herald*, 4 March 1943, both reproduced in McMurchy, Oliver and Thornley, *For Love or Money*, p. 122.
64 Reilly, 'The Rag Trade', p. 7.
65 Reilly, interview 1981.
66 Reilly, 'The Rag Trade', p. 8.
67 Reilly, interview 1981.
68 'Holiday Ban Ignored By Many Workers', *Sun News-Pictorial*, 26 December 1941, reproduced in Bolt, *Our Home Front*, p. 116; Darian-Smith, *On the Home Front*, p. 70.
69 Quoted in Beaton, 'The Importance of Women's Paid Labour', p. 72.
70 Mavis Robertson, 'Sally Bowen – Political and Social Experiences of a Working-Class Woman', First Women and Labour Conference, 1, p. 23.
71 Darian-Smith, *On the Home Front*, p. 64; Flo Davis, in Joyce Stevens, *Taking the Revolution Home*, p. 222.
72 Daphne Gollan, 'Memoirs of "Cleopatra Sweatfigure"', part 2, First Women and Labour Conference, extra papers, 2, p. 101.
73 *Round Table*, March 1945, quoted in Sheridan, *Mindful Militants*, p.

168.

74 'Cafe Waitresses Strike', *Sydney Morning Herald*, 9 September 1944, reproduced in McMurchy, Oliver and Thornley, *For Love or Money*, p. 122.

75 Information and quotes from James Hagan, 'Craft Power', in John Iremonger, John Merritt and Graeme Osborne (eds,), *Strikes: Studies in Twentieth Century Social History*, Sydney, Angus & Robertson, 1973, pp. 159-175.

76 Information on and quotes on women's voluntary work (unless otherwise specified) from Carmel Shute, '"The Second Line of Defence": Women's Voluntary War Work, 1939-1941', First Women and Labour Conference, extra papers 1, pp. 46-78, and the somewhat revised version of this article: 'From Balaclavas to Bayonets', pp. 5-26.

77 Interview with Hazel (Dobson) Donelly in Curlewis, 'Women Working in Heavy Industry', p. 469.

78 Shute, 'The Second Line of Defence', p. 68.

79 All information on this strike from Daphne Gollan, 'The Duly and Hansford Strike 1943: Find the Strikers', in Second Women and Labour Conference, pp. 341-348.

80 Andree Wright, 'Jessie Street, Feminist', in Curthoys, Eade and Spearrit, *Women at Work*, p. 64.

81 Ryan and Rowse, 'Women, Arbitration and the Family', p. 22.

82 Ryan and Rowse, 'Women, Arbitration and the Family', p. 25.

83 Gollan, 'Memoirs of "Cleopatra Sweatfigure"', p. 341.

4. Against the stream

1 *Our Women* (Union of Australian Women), Anniversary Issue, 1963, p. 24.

2 Betty Reilly, 'Winning the Women', *Communist Review*, May 1948, p. 209.

3 *Our Women*, September-December 1964, p. 12.

4 *The Sheet Metal Worker*, April 1943; February 1945; Ryan and Rowse, 'Women, Arbitration and the Family', p. 27.

5 Jessie Street, *Truth or Repose*, Sydney, Australasian Book Society, 1966, p. 124.

6 Janet Wakefield, 'Effects on Our Party of a Liberal Attitude Towards "Male Supremacy"', *Communist Review*, March 1953, p. 92.

7 *Queensland Guardian*, 16 May 1951.

8	*Guardian* (Victoria), 26 October and 5 November 1948.
9	*Tribune* (NSW), 10 March 1943; *Guardian*, 27 February 1948.
10	*Communist Review*, 5 May 1948, p. 142.
11	Daphne Gollan, personal interview, January 1979.
12	*Our Women*, Anniversary Issue, 1963, p. 22.
13	*Tribune*, 31 October 1956.
14	*Our Women*, Anniversary Issue, 1963, p. 24.
15	'Elizabeth', personal interview, October 1979.
16	Pat Elphinston, 'The Union of Australian Women', talk at the *Communists and the Labour Movement* Conference, August 1980, tape TMS 310, Latrobe Library, Melbourne.
17	Stella Nord, 'Women in Trade Unions', talk at the *Communists and the Labour Movement* Conference, August 1980, tape TMS 342-343, Latrobe Library, Melbourne.
18	Alice Hughes, 'Women in Trade Unions', talk at the *Communists and the Labour Movement* Conference, August 1980, tape TMS 342-343, Latrobe Library, Melbourne.
19	J. Penberthy, 'New Hand on Monday', *Our Women*, June-August 1969, pp. 4-6.
20	*Our Women*, March-May, 1956, p. 12.
21	Barbara Curthoys, 'International Women's Day in Newcastle in the Fifties and Sixties: A Personal Account', *Labour History*, vol. 66, May 1994, p. 126.
22	'Elizabeth', personal interview, October 1979.
23	Betty Olle, 'The Seventies Success Story – Women's Electoral Lobby', *Join Hands*, Communist Party of Australia, no 2, June 1973, p. 30.

5. Militant action among white collar workers

1	G. Gleghorn, *Life in General: A Short History of Organised Insurance Workers in Australia*, Melbourne, AIEU, n.d. [1991], p. 5.
2	Gleghorn, *Life in General*, pp. 29-31.
3	Commonwealth Arbitration Reports, vol. 127, pp. 1142-1160.
4	Commonwealth Arbitration Reports, vol. 127, p. 1158.
5	Australian Bureau of Statistics (ABS) 6306.0, *Distribution and composition of employee earnings and hours in Australia, 1975-1993*; ABS 6.22, *The labour force (historical supplement) 1964-1969*; ABS 6203.0, *The labour force Australia*; G. Griffin, *White Collar Militancy: The Australian*

Banking and Insurance Unions, Sydney, Croom Helm, pp. 60–61, 89–91; R. Lansbury, 'The Growth and Unionization of White-Collar Workers in Australia: Some Recent Trends', *Journal of Industrial Relations*, vol. 19, no. 1, March 1977, p. 48.

6 In 1971, 30.8 percent of the union's members were under 21 years old. On these points, see Griffin, *White Collar Militancy*, pp. 129, 140.

7 Griffin, *White Collar Militancy*, p. 87 (interview with Phil Reilly, December 1978).

8 *Special Premium*, no. 1, July 1972; *Premium*, July 1972; September 1973; AISF, *Industrial Newsletter*, n.d. [July 1972].

9 Interview with Marian Miller, 11 May 1995; interview with Kevin Davern, 3 October 1994.

10 AISF, FE minutes, 6 August 1973.

11 Griffin, *White Collar Militancy*, p. 158; AISF, Federal Executive (FE) minutes, 1 October 1973.

12 Griffin, *White Collar Militancy*, p. 68.

13 Report by Alleyn Best on meeting at RACV Insurance, 13 June, 1973 (collection of papers held by Phil Griffiths).

14 Militant Insurance Clerks [Phil Griffiths], *The fight for equal pay*, 1973, p. 3 (Griffiths papers).

15 Form letter, 1973 (Griffiths papers); Militant Insurance Clerks (MIC), 'Memo – Equal Pay', n.d. [August 1973]; McLeod-Best letters 16 and 21 August 1973 (both from Griffiths papers); AISF, FE minutes, 3 September 1973.

16 Griffin, *White Collar Militancy*, p. 68.

17 Interview with Kevin Davern, 3 October 1994.

18 Interview with Kevin Davern, 3 October 1994.

19 Interview with Phil Griffiths, 8 July 1995.

20 Interview with Phil Griffiths, 8 July 1995. Interestingly, a British study of women in insurance found this form of internalised sexism expressed by women in almost identical words. See Collinson and Knights, 'Men only', in D. Knights and H. Wilmott (eds.), *Gender and the Labour Process*, Macmillan, 1990, p. 161.

21 Interview with Marian Miller, 11 May 1995.

22 Interview with Elspeth McCracken-Hewson (employed at National Mutual in 1975), 11 May 1995.

23 AISF, Minutes of a meeting on equal pay, 25 September 1973 (Griffiths papers).

24 AISF, 'Equal pay campaign proposals', n.d. [?September 1973] (Griffiths papers).
25 *Clerk and Dagger* (5 October, 1973) claimed: 'it was not the male rank and file that dominated the meeting, it was the (male) general secretary, Ken McLeod. At the beginning of his talk he declared his desire to hear what women had to say, then rambled on for half an hour of the forty minute meeting...he ignored requests from the floor to finish speaking and allow discussion. He eventually responded by patronisingly announcing that what he had to say was important and the women should realise it.'
26 Gleghorn, *Life in General*, p. 81.
27 *Premium*, July 1973, pp. 26-27; by 2 October 1973, the AISF General Secretary was writing to all branch secretaries that 'equal pay is not a purely female issue. We need men to take part in a campaign if that became necessary, not merely because their support and numbers are needed but also because...male salaries...could also suffer. Growth in male membership should also be an aim in the context of an equal pay campaign.' (AISF, Z106, box 15, Noel Butlin Archives, ANU).
28 *Premium*, July 1973, p. 27.
29 *Premium*, November 1973; *Special Premium*, n.d. [November 1973]; 'AISF equal pay today' leaflet, 8 November 1973.
30 Interview with Phil Griffiths, 8 July 1995.
31 Commercial Union memorandum, 26 November 1973 (Griffiths papers).
32 AISF, FE minutes, 28 November and 3 December 1973.
33 AISF, FE minutes, 28 November 1973.
34 AISF, Minutes of mass meeting, 5 December 1973 (Griffiths papers); *Melbourne Herald*, 5 December 1973.
35 AISF, Victorian Branch Official Notice 'Equal pay strike this Friday 14 December' (Griffiths papers).
36 *Clerk and Dagger*, n.d. [December 1973]; *Premium*, February 1974.
37 *Special Premium*, n.d. [December 1973] (emphasis added); *Clerk and Dagger*, n.d. [December 1973].
38 Lansbury, 'The growth and unionization', pp. 47-48.
39 Griffin, *White Collar Militancy*, pp.18, 128; AISF, FE minutes, 22 January 1973; interview with Phil Griffiths, 8 July 1995.
40 AISF, President's report, 18 April 1973; interview with Phil Griffiths, 8 July 1995; interview with Kevin Davern, 3 October 1994; Griffin, *White*

Collar Militancy, p. 49. Membership increased in 1975, but this was largely due to the 'membership agreement' reached with the employers in August 1974, under which all new entrants into the insurance workforce had to join the AISF (Gleghorn, *Life in General*, p. 108). Given that the campaign directly addressed something specific to women, the other correlation that might be drawn is that between improved pay and conditions for women workers and increased female union membership. Unfortunately, the best that can be said of available figures for female membership of the insurance union is that they do not contradict this hypothesis. Data from the union show women increasing as a percentage of total membership from 37.3 percent in 1971 to 41.0 percent in 1973. Griffin, *White Collar Militancy*, p. 129; letter from General Secretary Ken McLeod to all branch secretaries, 2 October 1973 (Z106, box 15, Noel Butlin Archives, ANU).

41   Gleghorn, *Life in General*, p. 51; Griffin, *White Collar Militancy*; interview with Kevin Davern, 3 October 1994.
42   Interview with Phil Griffiths, 8 July 1995; *Premium*, vol. 25, no. 4, 1975.
43   *Miccy Finn*, 25 September 1973.
44   Gleghorn, *Life in General*, p. 104; AISF, President's report, AGM, 30 April 1974.
45   *Premium*, September 1968.
46   *Premium*, December 1973 (marked 'November' on cover).
47   M. Thornton, 'Equal pay in Australia', in F. Eyrand et al., *Equal Pay Protection in Industrialised Market Economies: In Search of Greater Effectiveness*, Geneva, International Labour Office, 1993, p. 26.
48   *Premium*, September–October 1962.
49   Lansbury, 'The growth and unionization', p. 48.

6. Sweatshop Rebels

This piece was based on personal experience and interviews intended for presentation at a non-academic forum, therefore records of sources were not kept. Participants in the strike continue to find the account here presented accurate.

7. Dedication doesn't pay the rent!

Quotes for which no references appear were taken from the author's notes and interviews, made at the time.

1 *The Battler*, 19 November 1983.
2 *The Age*, 11 October 1985.
3 *The Age*, 12 October 1985.
4 *Socialist Action*, November 1986.
5 *Socialist Action*, November 1986.
6 *The Age*, 18 October 1985.
7 *The Australian Financial Review*, 25 June 1986.
8 *Direct Action*, 5 November 1986.
9 *Direct Action*, 10 December 1986.
10 *Direct Action*, 3 December 1986; *The Age*, 12 November 1986.
11 *The Age*, 12 November 1986.
12 *Socialist Action*, February 1987.
13 *The Age*, 12 November 1986.
14 *The Age*, 12 December 1986.
15 *The Age*, 12 December 1986.
16 *Melbourne Herald*, 15 December 1986.
17 *The Age*, 17 December 1986.
18 *The Australian*, 27 December 1986.
19 *Direct Action*, 19 November 1986.
20 *Socialist Action*, December 1986.
21 *Melbourne Sun*, 18 November 1986.
22 *Melbourne Sun*, 12 November 1986.
23 *Socialist Action*, February 1987.

Image Credits

While every effort has been made to locate the copyright holders of images, the publisher welcomes hearing from anyone in this regard.

p. 12   Tom Mann addressing the crowd; view from the audience. Image reproduced with kind permission of Outback Archives, Broken Hill City Library, NSW.

p. 12   Tom Mann addressing the crowd; view from the stage. Image reproduced with kind permission of Outback Archives, Broken Hill City Library, NSW.

p. 15   Women marching in Mayday parade, Sydney 1933. Australian National University Library Archives online exhibition *Reds Under the Bed: 100 Years of Communism in Australia* (Z267 Box 29)

p. 18   Broken Hill Women's Memorial. Unknown artist. Photographer Janey Stone, September 2015

p. 21   The strike 1909: after the procession, 10 January 1909. Photographer Joseph Brokenshire (1877-1947). Broken Hill Outback Archives collection no. 91/3/357

p. 22   Broken Hill Strike Relief Committee, c.1910. Photographer unknown, Conlon Studio, Broken Hill. Image courtesy Broken Hill Outback Archives, collection no. 90/1/2003.

p. 24   1889 Barrier United Females Strike Protest Committee. Image reproduced with kind permission of Outback Archives, Broken Hill City Library, NSW.

p. 25   Cartoon depicting women assaulting strikebreakers. Image reproduced with kind permission of Outback Archives, Broken Hill City

	Library, NSW.
p. 26	Mrs Gibson. Image reproduced with kind permission of Outback Archives, Broken Hill City Library, NSW.
p. 27	Leaflet advertising speech by Adela Pankhurst on 'Women and War'. Image reproduced with kind permission of Outback Archives, Broken Hill City Library, NSW.
p. 30	Newspaper excerpt depicted on panel from permanent exhibition in the old Broken Hill Trades Hall. Details of newspaper article unknown. Photographer Janey Stone, September 2015
p. 31	Unemployed Union Women's Section. Image reproduced with kind permission of Outback Archives, Broken Hill City Library, NSW.
p. 32	'Leader of the Women's Brigade', cartoon (unknown cartoonist), 'The silver industry – sketches of the strike', *The Pictorial Australian* November–Christmas 1889, p. 161.
p. 35	Eight Hours Day Procession, Broken Hill, approximately 1911. Photographer Unknown. Ross and Keith Smith Collection, State Library of South Australia, ref. PRG 18/54/23a
pp. 36-37	Women's Brigade assisting the pickets during strike, 13 November 1889. Photographer George F. Jenkinson (1850–1923). Courtesy Broken Hill Outback Archives collection no. 94/3/17
pp. 38-39	Broken Hill public mural: 'Women Protestors'. Unknown artist. Photographer Janey Stone, September 2015
p. 42	Photograph, Wonthaggi miners demonstration with Women's Auxiliary, no date (1930s). Noel Butlin Archives Centre, Australian National University: Australasian Coal and Shale Employees' Federation, Edgar Ross collection, E165-56-180,
p. 44	'Fried Pegs', *Evening News* (Sydney) 9 January 1929, p. 1
p. 45	*Chronicle* (Adelaide) 26 January 1929, p.52
p. 46	'A Militant Woman', and 'But their Audience was Mostly Men', *Labor Daily* (Sydney) 7 March 1929, p. 1
p. 47	*The Woman Worker* 7 November 1928, p 1. Image: Reason in Revolt reasoninrevolt.com.au
p. 47	Militant Women's Movement of Australia rules and membership card, c. 1920s. Australian National University Library Archives online exhibition *Reds Under the Bed: 100 Years of Communism in Australia* (N336-68)
p. 48	Muriel Heagney, 'Lifelong Fight for Equal Pay', *The Sun* (Sydney) 24

IMAGE CREDITS

	July 1941, p. 13
pp. 50-51	South Maitland Unemployed Women's Bureau practising banner carrying for May Day 1930s. Image courtesy of Coalfields Local History Association Inc., digitised by Special Collections, University of Newcastle, Australia.
p. 55	Excerpt from 'Stay-in strike ends', *Burnie Advocate* 10 September 1938
p. 58	Picketing outside Paton and Baldwin Mill, Launceston, during the Lunch Hour, Monday 22 August 1932. Source: *Weekly Courier* (Launceston) 25 August 1932, p. 26. Courtesy of the State Library of Victoria.
p. 58	'Girl operatives outside Patons & Baldwins mill,' *Weekly Courier* (Launceston) 25 August 1932, 26. Courtesy of the State Library of Victoria.
p. 59	'E. Clarke, weaver at Kelsall and Kemp, 1930.' Photo in Miranda Morris-Nunn and C. B. Tassell, *Launceston's Industrial Heritage: A Survey*, QVMAG, 1982, p.189.
p. 59	'Crowd Listening to ATWU Tasmanian Branch Secretary Cyril Smith at the Rear of Trades Hall, Launceston, Monday morning 22 August 1932.' *Weekly Courier*, 25 August 1932, p. 26.
pp. 62-63	'A Group of Melbourne Textile Workers', *Working Woman,* September 1932.
p. 65	"Women's Rally," *Sydney Morning Herald*, 20 March 1929, p.17
p. 70	'Join us in a victory job'. Maurice Bramley, Department of National Service. Poster, Australian War Memorial ARTV00332
p. 70	*Australian Women's Weekly* 9 October 1943, front cover, source Trove. Image reproduced with kind permission of the Australian National Library.
p. 72	*'Won't you change your job for me?' Australian Women's Weekly* 17 April 1943, p. 2, source Trove. Image reproduced with kind permission of the Australian National Library.
p. 73	*'Miss 1941... helps to win the war,' Australian Women's Weekly* 31 May 1941, source Trove. Image reproduced with kind permission of the Australian National Library.
p. 75	Typescript letter from Jessie Street to the *Sydney Morning Herald* 1 September 1943. Image Reason in Revolt reasoninrevolt.com.au
p. 79	Women workers at the Commonwealth Aircraft Factory, Fisherman's Bend (Melbourne). Source: Australian War Memorial, ref.

	045372
p. 80	Women munition factory workers. Photographer unknown. State Library of Victoria (H98.105/714A)
p. 81	Miss Mildred Thornton at a lathe in machine shop. Photographer unknown. State Library of Victoria (H98.105/717)
p. 86	'Munitions women cease work', Melbourne *Argus* 23 May 1944 p. 3
p. 89	'Metal union will support strike by women', *Sunday Telegraph* 28 February 1944, p. 5
p. 91	'The textile girl on strike', *Sunday Sun* 14 November 1942, p. 6
p. 92	'Police called out; city textile mills patrolled', *The Sun* 4 September 1944, p. 3
p. 93	Betty Reilley c. 1950s. Australian National University Library Archives online exhibition *Reds Under the Bed: 100 Years of Communism in Australia* (N188-4-2)
p. 94	'400 waitresses on strike', *Daily Telegraph* 9 September 1944, p. 5
p. 94	'City girls strike'/'Leaflet raid by strikers', *The Sun* 8 February 1943, p. 3
p. 98	'Women bitter about strikers', *Daily Telegraph* 19 July 1943, p. 7
p. 99	'K.C.'s wife gives evidence on war factory strike', *The Sun* 18 June 1943, p. 3
p. 102	Union of Australian Women demonstration over equal pay early 1960s. Photographer Zillah Lee. Courtesy of Anne Sgro.
pp. 104-105	*Guardian* 12 November 1948. Published with kind permission of the Search Foundation.
p. 106	*The New Housewife*, no. 5, April 1949. Image Reason in Revolt reasoninrevolt.net.au. Published with kind permission of Anne Sgro.
p. 107	Photographer unknown. New Housewives' Association demonstration 1950s, Russell St Melbourne. Courtesy Anne Sgro.
p. 108-109	Photograph, Women's Auxiliary holding placard, no date. Noel Butlin Archives Centre, Australian National University: Australasian Coal and Shale Employees' Federation, Edgar Ross collection, E165-56-10
p. 111	Still images from *Hewers of Coal* (WWFFU, 1957). Images courtesy of National Film and Sound Archive and Maritime Union of Australia.
pp. 112-115	Still images from Waterside Workers' Federation Film News No.1 (WWWFFU, 1956). Images courtesy of National Film and Sound Archive and Maritime Union of Australia.

IMAGE CREDITS

pp. 118-119	Union of Australian Women demonstration. Photographer unknown. Courtesy of Anne Sgro.
pp. 120-121	Union of Australian Women demonstration over maternity allowance. Photographer unknown. Courtesy of Anne Sgro.
p. 122	New Housewives' Association flyer about price rises late 1940s. Image reproduced with kind permission of Anne Sgro.
pp. 124-127	Union of Australian Women demonstration over equal pay early 1960s. Photographer Zillah Lee. Courtesy of Anne Sgro.
p. 130	Newcastle International Women's Day demonstrations 1948, 1963 and 1964. *Newcastle International Women's Day Celebrations 1944-2011*, University of Newcastle Special Collections
p. 132	'Equal Pay Protest, Melbourne Town Hall, Melbourne, Victoria, 20 Feb 1969'. Photographer Laurie Richards. Museums Victoria Collections. https://collections.museumsvictoria.com.au/items/797664. Accessed 29 March 2022
pp. 138-139	International Women's Day Sydney 1975. Photographer Anne Roberts. Mitchell Library, State Library of New South Wales and Courtesy SEARCH Foundation
p. 147	*Clerk and Dagger*, no. 2, 8 November 1972. Reproduced with kind permission of Phil Griffiths.
p. 154	Photographer unknown. *The Battler* 23 January 1982, p. 10.
pp. 158-159	Photographer unknown. *The Battler* 23 January 1982, p. 10.
p. 160	Photographer unknown. *The Battler* 23 January 1982, p. 10.
p. 161	*Migration Action (Publication of the Ecumenical Migration Centre), Vol. VI Number 2. 1982, front cover.*
p. 162	*Artist unknown, untitled. Migration Action (Publication of the Ecumenical Migration Centre), Vol. VI Number 2. 1982, p. 51.*
p. 165	*The Kortex factory partly demolished in 2021. Photographer Belle Gibson.*
p. 168	*Collage of images from the 1986 nurses' strike, digital painting by Sage Jupe. Published with kind permission of Sage Jupe.*
p. 170	'Vic nurses strike over award', *Tribune* 5 November 1986, p.4. Published with kind permission of the Search Foundation.
p. 171	'Nurses defiant', *The Sun* 8 November 1986
p. 172	Australian Nursing and Midwifery Federation, *The 1986 50-day Victorian nurses and midwives strike* (online feature), https://otr.anmfvic.asn.au/articles/the-1986-50-day-victorian-nurses-and-midwives-strike

p. 177	'Solid support for nurses as dispute widens', *Tribune* 19 November 1986, p. 5. Image reproduced with kind permission of the Search Foundation.
p. 178	Two images from photographer Maggie Diaz. State Library of Victoria ID 2972618. Published with kind permission of Gwendoline de Lacey, Curator Maggie Diaz collection.
p. 182	Australian Nursing and Midwifery Federation, *The 1986 50-day Victorian nurses and midwives strike* (online feature), https://otr.anmfvic.asn.au/articles/the-1986-50-day-victorian-nurses-and-midwives-strike.
p. 183	'Nurses solid despite government attacks', *Tribune* 3 December 1986, p.7. Published with kind permission of the Search Foundation.
p. 184	'Nurses holding firm after seven weeks', *Tribune* 17 December 1986. Published with kind permission of the Search Foundation.

Contributors

SANDRA BLOODWORTH became a socialist in the 1970s Civil Liberties struggle against the Bjelke-Petersen government in Queensland. She was active in the Kortex strike chronicled in this book. Currently on the *Marxist Left Review* editorial committee, Sandra has written on women's liberation; Marx and Engels on gender oppression; Lenin; and unions' support for Aboriginal rights.

DIANE FIELDES began her life as a socialist in the movement against the Vietnam War and remains a Marxist activist today. She has been involved in campaigns from the anti-apartheid movement to the fight to free the refugees and was a long-term union delegate at work. Now retired, she writes for Socialist Alternative's newspaper *Red Flag* and the *Marxist Left Review* while helping to organise with new generations of revolutionaries.

TOM O'LINCOLN joined the radical student movement in Germany in 1967 and was subsequently a socialist organiser, unionist, journalist and writer. One major interest has been the CPA, and he is the author of *Into the Mainstream: The Decline of Australian Communism*. His political memoir, *The Highway is for Gamblers*, covers his life as a political activist for 50 years in the USA, Germany, Australia and Indonesia. Currently living in residential care, Tom continues his commitment to revolutionary Marxism.

LIZ ROSS joined Women's Liberation and Gay Liberation in Canberra in the early 1970s and later wrote *Revolution is for Us! The Left and Gay Liberation in Australia*. In the 1980s, she was a union delegate in the public service. A supporter of the BLF, she wrote *Dare to Struggle, Dare to Win: Builders Labourers Fight Deregistration, 1981–84*. Experience of this and the 1986 nurses strike, as well as other union struggles in the 1980s and 1990s, resulted in her latest book, *Stuff the Accord! Pay Up! Workers' Resistance to the ALP–ACTU Accord*. She moved from movement to socialist politics in 1978, remaining actively involved to the present and is now with Socialist Alternative.

JANEY STONE became a socialist in 1962, participating in student and antiwar campaigns. She joined the Women's Liberation Movement in 1969. Since then, she has been a union delegate, political activist and frequent writer in many fields, including women workers; sexual politics; and the Middle East. Her most recent field of research and publication is the radical Jewish tradition. Janey continues her activity in retirement through Interventions. She edited this new version of *Rebel Women* and is editing the revised editions of Tom O'Lincoln's published works.

About Interventions

Interventions is an independent, not-for-profit, incorporated publisher. We publish left-wing, radical and socialist books by Australian authors. We welcome books which, for political or financial reasons, commercial publishers are unlikely to accept. Our books cover a wide range of topics, including labour history, left-wing politics, radical cultural themes, socialism and Marxism, memoirs and works about resistance to racism, sexism and all other forms of oppression.

At Interventions, we believe that radical ideas matter. We want our books to be part of the development of a critical and engaged Australian left.

By highlighting alternative voices, especially those who have been pushed to the margins, we hope to contribute to a greater insight and awareness of the injustices that exist in society and the many grassroots efforts to right these wrongs.

See all our books at **https://interventions.org.au/books**

We welcome publishing proposals. If you are interested in submitting a proposal, please check out the specific information for authors on our website: **https://interventions.org.au/forauthors**. If you believe that your proposal fits our guidelines, please follow the submission process outlined there. Please note that we are not currently publishing poetry or fiction.

Interventions has no independent source of income and is committed to keeping prices accessible. As bookshops and warehouses close around the world, our future hangs in the balance. By supporting us, you will help us to keep radical ideas alive and accessible to all. If you would like to support radical publishing in Australia, please consider supporting our Patreon. Visit patreon.com/interventions to donate a small amount each month and get some great rewards.

Website: **https://interventions.org.au/**

Contact us: **info@interventions.org.au** or use the contact form on the website.

About this book

The Interventions editor and production project manager for this book was Janey Stone. Sandra Bloodworth, Diane Fieldes, Lisa Milner and Liz Ross also contributed.

Eris Jane Harrison AE of Effective Editing copy edited this book. Eris is a freelance editor accredited by the Institute of Professional Editors Australia (IPEd). She is a member of IPEd and the Canberra Society of Editors (CSE).

Belle Gibson of Dicey Design designed and laid out this book. Belle has experience and training in a range of both print and digital design formats. She specialises in publishing-related design. Access more of her work at **dicey.design** or contact her via **belloudesign@gmail.com**.

— ALSO BY INTERVENTIONS —

WITHOUT BOSSES
Radical Australian Trade Unionism in the 1970s
by Sam Oldman

'The book demonstrates that labour militancy and the practice of worker control is not an antediluvian form but a compelling force with a powerful legacy in the present... activists today should take heart in the fact that the urge for workers' power is never far from the surface.'
Immanuel Ness, Professor of Political Science, City University of New York

Without Bosses gives a fascinating insight into radical currents in Australian trade unionism which pushed the boundaries of action during the 1970s. Trail-blazing actions include the mass strikes against the penal powers in 1969 and the famous green bans of the Builders Labourers' Federation in the following years. The book also details less well-known but fascinating experiments. At factories, coal mines and building sites across the country, workers 'sacked' their managers and supervisors, took over their workplaces and ran them without bosses. These measures were a radical departure from the traditionally recognised activities of trade unions. Without Bosses overflows with incredible and inspiring stories from a critically important period in Australian history. For anyone interested in labour history, left-wing ideas, and the power of unions, it is required reading.

ALSO BY INTERVENTIONS

REVOLUTION IS FOR US
The left and gay liberation in Australia
Liz Ross

'The homosexual is essential to the sexual revolution; there can be no revolution, no liberation, without us.'

Australia's Gay Liberation movement arose at a time when revolution was in the air and gays wanted to be part of it. It was the Left which had a theory and practice of revolution – Marxism. But it is often asserted that the Left was backward and even hostile, that Marxism had no tradition of dealing with sexual oppression. This book challenges those claims and shows that the Left – and the working class – was involved in the earliest gay rights movements and was integral to the new Gay Liberation Movement. It also refutes the claim that the Left has no intellectual tools to explain the oppression of women and gays. The book uncovers the rich history of the Left and Gay Liberation in Australia, an inspiration for activists today.

— ALSO BY INTERVENTIONS —

RADICAL PERTH, MILITANT FREMANTLE
edited by Charlie Fox, Alexis Vassiley, Bobbie Oliver, and Lenore Layman

Radical Perth, Militant Fremantle tells 34 fascinating stories of radical moments In the cities' past, from as long ago as the 1890s and as recent as Occupy: the revolutionary theatre of the Workers Art Guild; the riot of unemployed workers outside the Treasury building; rock concerts inside St Georges Cathedral; bodgies and widgies cutting up the dance floor at the Scarborough Beach Snake Pit; the Point Peron women's peace camp, and many more.

This revised 2nd edition bring four new tales: student radicalism at Curtin University (then WAIT), Perth's very-own Green Bans; Perth solidarity with the famous strike of Aboriginal pastoral workers; and the unknown tale of striking Chinese seamen on the Fremantle waterfront, who faced brutal repression, but won support from Fremantle unionists.

This engaging, inspiring book charts Perth and Fremantle's radical past, uncovering the obscure and neglected, reframing the better known, opening new windows on Perth and Fremantle's history. It is structured as three self-guided walking and driving tours, so readers can visit the very places and buildings where these hidden histories took place.

www.ingramcontent.com/pod-product-compliance
Lightning Source LLC
Chambersburg PA
CBHW071959290426
44109CB00018B/2071